five things I did
right&
five things I did
wrong
in raising our children

five things I did
right &
five things I did
wrong

in raising our children

Sarah O. Maddox

BROADMAN
&HOLMAN
PUBLISHERS

NASHVILLE, TENNESSEE

0-8054-3142-X

Published by Broadman & Holman Publishers
Nashville, Tennessee

Dewey Decimal Classification: 649
Subject Heading: MOTHER AND CHILD \
CHILD REARING \ PARENTING

Scripture quotations are taken from the following: NIV, New International Version, copyright © 1973, 1978, 1984 by International Bible Society; NASB, New American Standard Bible, © 1960, 1962, 1963, 1968, 1971, 1972, 1973, 1975, 1977, 1995 by the Lockman Foundation. Used by permission.; NKJV, New King James Version, copyright © 1979, 1980, 1982, Thomas Nelson, Inc., Publishers; NLT, New Living Translation, copyright © 1996. Used by permission of Tyndale House Publishers, Inc., Wheaton, Illinois 60189. All rights reserved.; and KJV, King James Version.

1 2 3 4 5 6 7 8 09 08 07 06 05 04

Acknowledgments

First I would like to acknowledge eight men who greatly impacted the contents of this book. My husband, Roland, who has unreservedly loved and supported me through all the years of our marriage and has continually lived before his children an exemplary life; my father, the late Dr. Joe T. Odle, a godly minister and religious writer who was an inspiration to his family and to all who knew him; Dr. Adrian P. Rogers, my pastor for over twenty years, whose consistent example and faithful and forceful proclamation of the Word of God served as a strong bulwark to our family; Dr. James Dobson, whose timely insights and counsel to Christian families were a constant help throughout our parenting years; Bill Gothard, whose Institute in Basic Youth Conflicts was a godsend to us and to our teenagers; Dr. Gary Smalley and Dr. John Trent, whose books *The Blessing* and *The Gift of Honor* encouraged us greatly in the area of "blessing" our children; and Josh McDowell, whose teachings continually affirmed the standards which we had set for our kids. In very different ways, each of these men profoundly influenced me in the positive aspects of my child training. To all of them, I shall be eternally grateful.

Second, I owe a deep debt of gratitude to a special group of friends who are also experts in the field of child development: to Dr. Chuck Hannaford, outstanding Christian psychologist, who graciously critiqued my manuscript and encouraged me to submit it to the publisher; and to those nine who responded to my questionnaire, allowing me to use their valuable insights and timeless wisdom in this book. They are Nancy (Mrs. Les) Binkley, Pat (Mrs. Charles) Brand,

Patty (Mrs. David) Hankins, Rev. and Mrs. Rob Mullins, Peggy (Mrs. Jay) Perkins, Dr. and Mrs. Van Snider, and Ruth Ann (Mrs. Wayne) VanderSteeg.

A special thanks is reserved for my excellent editors, Leonard Goss and Kim Overcash; and my great assistant, Kathy Douglass, who worked many hours in order to secure the permissions I needed. To all of these,
I offer my deep appreciation. I shall always be grateful for your special contribution to this book.

Dedication

I dedicate this book to our beloved children:
Melanie Kendall Maddox Redd
Thomas Alan Maddox

Table of Contents

Foreword

I'm not certain exactly when it happened, but some-where along the way I realized that the home I had grown up in was unique. Up until that point, I suppose that I thought my home, my parents, my upbringing, and my church were just the norm. I assumed that everyone else out there was just like us, or at least somewhat like us.

However, conversations began to take place that awakened me to the possibility that everyone else was not just like us. I'd hear a girl share about all of her parents' fights, another tell of her dad's many affairs, and even another share about the cruel abuse she had suffered at the hand of someone she trusted. Possibility became reality. The home that I was raised in was not only unique, it was absolutely an exception to any norm you might set.

I can remember thinking and sometimes saying things like:

"You mean your parents never . . ."

"You guys were allowed to do what?"

"In your home, I can't believe you never prayed together."

"I thought everyone was taken to church on Sunday."

"You mean you never owned a Bible?"

"Are you sure your mom and dad didn't encourage you in some way?"

"Your parents let you hang out with whomever you wanted?"

Honestly, I was shocked when I first learned that we were really different from a lot of other families. But as the years have passed by and I have gotten older, I know now that we were one of the most unusual families around. I assumed so many things were just the norm; yet, I was wrong.

And for my very different and unusual family, I am grateful. I'm thankful that my parents and grandparents stepped out of the culturally acceptable way of thinking and dared to be different. I'm blessed that they didn't settle for less than the best.

When I consider the things they did that I am most grateful for, I can lay it out in five family certainties:

1. Without a doubt, I knew my parents loved each other.

2. Without a doubt, our family was going to go to church together! Church was never an option; it was part of who we were and what we did.

3. Without a doubt, prayer and God's Word mattered most in our home. These were the two spiritual disciplines that could take you through any crisis.

4. Without a doubt, we were going to be prayed for by both of our parents—daily.

5. Without a doubt, my parents practiced the morals that they preached.

Although our family was not perfect and my parents were not saints, there were a lot of things done right in our home. We had our hard moments, our arguments and stresses, and our tough days. Yet my brother and I had great role models, and our lives are testimonies to that fact. This book is a testimony from my mom as to what she felt she did, both right and wrong, in her child raising. As I have read through her insights, I agree with and support what she has written. I believe my parents did the best they knew how to do. I am grateful for all of the energy, time, prayers, attention, tears, and heart they poured into my life.

As you read through this book, you will find Scriptures and practical instruction from my mom as well as a word or two from me. My prayer is that you will not find a family to put on a pedestal, but rather a living testimony that loudly proclaims the fact that God is faithful! God bless you and your home as you read.

—Melanie Kendall Maddox Redd

Introduction

At a Christian gathering in New Orleans, Louisiana, in June 2001, I was engaged in a conversation with a younger friend of mine. Not surprisingly, our conversation turned to children and grandchildren. As we talked, I heard myself sharing some things I felt that I, as a mother, had done wrong in the raising of our children. We ended the time together with my saying, "I guess I just need to write a book about all the things I did wrong in raising my kids." I laughed, and we both moved on to other conversations.

As I left the room that night, my heart was suddenly heavy. So many memories paraded across my mind, most of them negative. *Why did I focus on those experiences with my friend?* I asked myself. *Why didn't I just share good things? Why should I write a book about my mistakes?*

My mind wandered back to the many times young mothers had asked, "Sarah, if you could go back in time, what would you do differently in your child raising?" For a long time I really had not known how to answer their question, but that night in New Orleans, God impressed upon my heart that a book about my "mistakes" might be helpful to young mothers—it might prevent them from making the same mistakes I felt I had made. Almost immediately God reminded me that not everything I did concerning my children was wrong. By his grace I had done a lot of things right. I should share both the positive and the negative aspects of my days of mothering.

That night this book, *Five Things I Did Right and Five Things I Did Wrong in Raising Our Children,* began to materialize. I prayed and agonized over it. I knew

I could not write it without God's blessing or the permission of my family. Now, several years later, I do believe writing this book was a part of God's plan for me. I gladly give it to you, dear reader. May you learn from its pages that which will help you avoid some of my missteps. I pray that on the positive side, you will be inspired, as God leads, to put into practice—in teaching and training your children—some of the things I would not change.

Today both of my children are faithfully serving the Lord. I praise God for that! They have turned out well in spite of my mistakes, and your children can too. None of us is a perfect parent. God, our heavenly Father, is the only perfect parent. Yet with his guidance and direction, we earthly, imperfect parents can be more of what he desires us to be. Look to the Lord all the days of your life. He will never fail you or forsake you. God says: "I will instruct you and teach you in the way which you should go; I will counsel you with My eye upon you" (Ps. 32:8 NASB).

section one

five things i
did wrong

If a child lives with approval,
he learns to live with himself.

DOROTHY LAW NOLTE, *GOD'S LITTLE DEVOTIONAL BOOK FOR MOMS*

Chapter 1

I Didn't Praise My Children Enough

> ∽
>
> Therefore, accept one another, just as Christ also accepted us to the glory of God.
>
> ROMANS 15:7 NASB
>
> ∽

I stood on the observation deck of my life, peering through the "retrospective lens" that had taken me back in time. As the scenes paraded by one by one, I fast-forwarded to my days of motherhood and child raising. Momentarily, I paused to ask myself, *Why am I so anxious to review this phase of my life? Wasn't it often difficult for me?* And yet, so many young women I had met through the years had asked the thought-provoking question: "What would you do differently in your child raising if you could go back in time?" How could I answer without some reflection?

With their question looming in the forefront of my mind, I permitted the "picture show" to move forward. It was an intriguing and somewhat scary thing to do, but my curiosity would not allow me to do otherwise.

As that eventful period came into focus, familiar snapshots began to flash into view: birthdays, school days, sports events, church choir trips, broken relationships, hurt feelings—joyful occasions and not-so-joyful occasions, all marching in a colorful procession. They soon formed a collage, sticking together in the pages of my "memory book." Some pictures were very clear; others were fuzzy. Some were quite pleasant to remember; others produced unpleasant memories accompanied by feelings I didn't relish experiencing again.

But isn't that what life is like for all of us? Some of it is pleasant; some of it is painful. Some days you wish could be repeated; others you would like to erase.

One thing was crystal clear, however—God had been exceedingly good to me and to my family through all those years. He had unmessed my messes more times than I could count. He had written Romans 8:28—"And we know that all things work together for good to them that love God, to them who are the called according to his purpose" (KJV)—on page after page of my memory album. I had so much for which to be thankful!

What could I learn from looking back on all those experiences? What value would peering through that special "lens" provide? Would my observations be of help to other mothers? My conclusion was "yes." If I would be transparent, perhaps today's young mothers could learn from my mistakes and benefit from my insights.

Praise and Affirmation

One of the first insights gleaned from this "viewing" was a conviction that I had not praised my children enough—I had not affirmed them suffi-ciently. I also realized that my own upbringing had played a vital role in the way I related to my children. As a mother it had been my earnest desire to love my children unconditionally and affirm them in ways that would be meaningful and beneficial to their development. I knew that God's love toward us, his children, is unconditional and that our love for our children is also to be unconditional—we are to love them unreservedly, just as God loves us. However, because I had not been given adequate praise and val-idation in *my* growing up years, verbalizing my love for my children did not come easily for me.

Throughout the first twenty years of my life I fre-quently longed for my mother's approval. She was a wonderful, godly lady who loved me dearly, but she seemed to be afraid to give me words of praise or com-mendation. Although I believe she was truly proud of my accomplishments, I never heard it from her lips. My natural conclusion, therefore, was to assume that I did not measure up to her expectations. As a result, my self-image was low. I learned many years later that my maternal grandmother had passed on to Mother the belief that praising one's children would give them the "big head"—filling them with pride. Mother obviously adopted that belief as her own and prac-ticed it for a long, long time.

When I went off to college, however, something happened: Mother did a 180-degree turn. She began to praise me for every little thing I accomplished. In fact, it was almost embarrassing. Sadly, although her words of affirmation continued for the rest of her life, the damage of those first twenty years was hard for me to overcome.

As a result of what I had personally experienced, I decided I was not going to relate to my own children in the same manner; I was going to praise my children appropriately *all* of their lives. Even so, my best endeavors were not sufficient. I knew they needed my words of encouragement and acceptance; however, it seemed I often focused more on the negative than on the positive. I now see that there were several parenting pitfalls I was not prepared to handle.

Compliant Children

First of all, I misjudged the needs of my compliant daughter. She was so easy to raise, so anxious to please. She continually did things that made us proud of her. For some reason, however, I did not praise her adequately—I did not give her enough of the positive reinforcement she needed. Obviously, I was not aware of her needs or I would have changed my behavior. When the truth of the situation came to my attention in later years, I asked her forgiveness for my failure to adequately commend her model behavior and good works.

As I have studied other families through the years, I believe it is a common practice for parents to fail to praise sufficiently the child who is easy to raise—the one who is responsive to authority, does not cause a parent "grief," and is often a model child. The reasons may be diverse, but the practice is the same. Although parents are grateful to have such a child, they sometimes forget the importance of verbally expressing their gratitude to him or her.

Our compliant children need words of affirmation and approval. They need words of praise to encourage them in their obedience and right living. It is vital for them to know that their parents appreciate their good behavior. If mom and dad are so occupied with a high-maintenance child, or perhaps with several other siblings, that the low-maintenance son or daughter does not get the validation he or she needs, this can result in a build-up of anger and resentment toward the other sibling(s) and perhaps toward the parents too.

The Elder Brother Syndrome

This phenomenon has been given a name: it is called the "elder brother" syndrome. The title is taken from the parable Jesus told concerning the prodigal son. In this parable a man's younger son asked for his inheritance early and left home, going to live in a distant country. While there, he squandered his money in wild living. Finding himself destitute and "at the end of his rope," he determined that being a hired servant for his father would be better than living in his present condition. When the prodigal son returned home, his daddy was elated to see him and welcomed him with open arms. Additionally, the father killed the fatted calf, held a banquet in his son's honor, and rewarded him with a gold ring. The elder brother, however, did not respond well to this out-pouring of love from his father to his younger, prodigal brother. He evidently felt that he had been a good son all along. He was so resentful and unhappy with the attention showered on his brother, he refused to attend the homecoming celebration.

I believe this "elder brother" syndrome can be present in a home whether there is a prodigal or not. All that is necessary is the absence of spoken words of blessing and affirmation. In their excellent book *The Blessing,* Gary Smalley and John Trent tell us: "If you are a parent, your children desperately need to hear a spoken blessing from you. . . . Spoken words of blessing should start in the delivery room and continue throughout life."[1]

"Bless Me, My Father!"

The Bible also tells the story of Jacob stealing his father's "blessing," which rightfully belonged to his brother Esau. When Esau learned of this terrible betrayal, Scripture tells us he cried with an exceedingly great and bitter cry, and said to his father, "Bless me—me also, O my father!" (Gen. 27:38 NKJV). His father, Isaac, informed him: "Your brother came with deceit and has taken away your blessing" (v. 35). In great consternation, Esau exclaimed, "Have you only one blessing, my father? Bless me—me also" (v. 38). Then he began to weep again.

Although today's father may not give to his firstborn the same type of blessing given in Old Testament times, it is absolutely essential to give our children the great blessing of knowing that they are loved unconditionally by their parents. Verbalizing words of blessing is vital. Many times we have heard people say, "I never heard my father *tell* me he loved me." How tragic! We do not want this to happen in the lives of our own children.

Maxine Marsolini says: "An effective parent . . . learns how to celebrate each child and give him a sense of value, so that one day he will be an influential person in his own world. He will be equipped to spread godliness into another generation and the blessing baton will pass on into the future."[2] Whether the child is compliant or noncompliant, he needs to hear often from his parents that he is a valuable member of their household—that he is someone to celebrate! If he is to pass on the "blessing baton," he must first receive our blessing.

The High-Maintenance Child

For the child who is high maintenance, a parent may have to seek out opportunities to affirm and praise him. Because the negative things in his life seem to outweigh the positive ones, this is sometimes difficult. One pediatrician suggested to a mother that in order to be more positive and less negative with her son, she should write the words *Praise him* on three-by-five-inch cards. These cards would inspire her to praise the Lord as well as her child. She was to attach these cards to her bathroom mirror and kitchen window as constant reminders that this son needed her praise. He needed to know for certain that his parents loved him. Expressing love through words of affirmation and support was absolutely essential for his emotional health.

"I'll Never Measure Up"

Just as the "elder brother" syndrome is a common phenomenon in homes across the land, there is another syndrome found frequently in today's success-oriented families: the "I'll never measure up" syndrome. First, there's the underachiever whose siblings are achievers. He can easily become discouraged about his failure to succeed, feeling that he may never measure up to his brother's or sister's achievements. This discouragement can lead to depression, apathy about schoolwork, or other negative behaviors. Then there's the child who feels he can never measure up to his parents' expectations of him. Even if he tries to please

11

them, he does not receive the positive strokes and commendation he so desperately needs and desires from his mother and dad.

Both of these types of struggling children can give up on *ever* gaining approval at home. They may begin to look for acceptance outside their homes, finding it all too frequently among the wrong crowd. When warning signs begin to appear, I believe parents need to take stock of the situation and ask, "Is our child receiving the validation he needs from us? Does he feel he must find his positive strokes elsewhere?" It behooves a parent to seek to communicate love and genuine acceptance to the struggling child.

Praising the Difficult Child

A parent may ask, "For what can I praise my child who is struggling?" "How do I affirm my high-maintenance or 'difficult' child?" I suggest the following:

1. *Pray for wisdom.* Ask God to show you how you can affirm your child and make him feel accepted in your family. Smalley and Trent remind us: "Children who grow up with a strong sense of belonging gain ground on those who don't. The seeds of acceptance that are sown in children who feel they belong will bear fruit in giving them the ability to give and receive love and acceptance later in life."[3]

2. *Search for the good.* Make every effort to catch your child doing something good. Actively look for the good things he is doing. Some of his behavior will be positive, no matter his age or stage.

3. *Accentuate the positive.* Ignore as many of the little negative behaviors as you honestly feel you can. Concentrate on what your child is doing right. If

you compliment what he does right, he will be more likely to repeat that good behavior in the future. Dr. Charles Stanley once said, "The greatest motivation in the world for learning is praise. . . . If you want your children to do right things, praise them for even the smallest things they do right."[4]

4. *"Paint" him a picture.* Even if your child is not currently behaving as you would like, picture the future for him as you think it could be. This idea also comes from *The Blessing,* by Smalley and Trent. In explaining this principle, the authors say, "Picturing a special future for a child can help bring out the best in their lives. It gives them a positive direction to strive toward."[5] They go on to say, "When a person feels in his or her heart that the future is hopeful and something to look forward to, it can greatly affect his or her attitude on life. In this way we are providing our children . . . with a clear light for their path in life."[6]

For example, if your child is good with his hands, you might say to him, "You may be an electrician or engineer someday; you are so good at putting things together." Or if he is a strong-willed child, you could predict: "I just believe you are going to be a real leader someday." For a little girl who loves children, you might say, "You are going to be a great mother!" In all these instances you are planting hopeful and positive thoughts in the child's mind and heart.

When our son Alan was growing up, I often felt led by the Lord to tell him that he was going to make a good daddy. I didn't know why God was leading me to do this, but he was, and I obeyed him. Today I am happy to say that Alan indeed is a wonderful daddy. One way God prepared him for this task was through "pictures" of his future.

Several years ago a young mother related this story to me. Her two-year-old had begun to use bad words. Evidently he had heard them in the neighborhood, because his parents never talked that way at home. The parents' correcting and scolding seemed to be of no avail. They were devastated, wondering what they should do. After earnestly praying about this situation, one of the things God led them to do was to picture a notable future for their little boy. On a regular basis the mother started telling her little son, "Someday you are going to be a mighty man of God!"

The bad words decreased somewhat by the time he turned three years old, but not altogether. His parents continued to pray and picture a positive future for him. When he was four and out shopping with his mother, something quite significant happened. In a particular store, the little boy wandered a few feet from his mother. A lady nearby began talking with him. The mother carefully observed them. In a moment she overheard the lady ask her son an often-asked question: "What are you going to be when you grow up?" Without hesitation the little boy answered, "A mighty man of God!" And his mother believes with all her heart that's exactly what her son will be.

5. *Intercede for him.* Pray that God will work in your child's life to make him more worthy of praise—that he will become the person God desires for him to be. Philippians 2:13 says: "For it is God who is at work in you, both to will and to work for His good pleasure" (NASB). Pray that God will do this work so that your child will develop strong beliefs and convictions and bring pleasure and glory to the Savior.

Be certain that as his parent, *you* are setting an example of godliness—that you are seeking to live in obedience to God's commands. First John 2:6 states: "The one who says he abides in Him ought himself to walk in the same manner as He [Jesus] walked" (NASB). Dr. Stanley applied this to parenting when he said, "There is nothing under heaven like a mother and a father patterning principles they believe in if they want to hand those principles down to their children."[7]

Looking Back

If I could go back in time, I would speak the message of love and acceptance more clearly and more often to both of my children. I would seek to praise them generously. I would try to "celebrate each child," being certain both *knew* that I valued them highly—that they were my "priceless treasures" from the Lord. Vicki Mullins, a minister's wife and mother of two, stated, "Legitimate praise is important. A child needs to know that the parent is standing with him and behind him. They [his parents] are the child's support, foundation, and cheerleader."[8]

In the book *The Gift of Honor,* Smalley and Trent emphasize the importance of communicating love to our children: "Genuine love is a gift we give others. It isn't purchased by their actions or contingent upon our emotions at the moment. It may carry with it strong emotional feelings, but it isn't supported by them. Rather, it is a *decision* we make on a daily basis that someone is special and valuable to us. . . . When we give our children the gift of honor—that is, when we learn how to communicate to them in tangible ways that they are deeply loved and highly

15

valued—it goes a long way toward combating future problems in their lives."[9]

What we value, we handle very carefully. Where our children are concerned, sensitivity is called for in handling their emotional needs. They need to feel secure in our love. Patty Hankins, mother of three successful adult sons, states, "I believe security is the emotional thread that ties our love, our time, our praise, our prayers together. Where there are gaps, it fills those in. When it is missing, all other things are shaky."[10] Our kids need to *know* how valuable they are to us, their parents—they need to *feel* loved. This verbal communication of love is given in the knowledge that the absence of such words of blessing can result in problems we do not want our children to have. Remember: "Both people and relationships suffer in the absence of spoken words of love, encouragement and support."[11]

As Vicki Mullins states, "Everyone needs to know someone loves them with no strings attached. They need unconditional acceptance—they need to know that they are important and 'enough' as they are."[12] This will not come without a spoken message—a message of love and caring—said often and in many different ways. And we should remember: It won't hurt to compliment our children in public when they are really deserving of commendation.

Honoring Our Children, Not Worshipping Them

A word of caution must be inserted at this point: Honoring our children by communicating to them that they are greatly loved and truly valued must not be confused with treating our offspring as little gods. We are not to worship our children. We must differentiate between making certain a child knows he is loved and making him or her an "idol" in our lives. In the context of loving one's children, some parents attempt to convey their love through overindulgence and "child worship." I asked Dr. Van Snider, Associate Clinical Professor of Pediatrics at the University of Tennessee Center for Health Sciences, Memphis, Tennessee, what concerned him most about today's mothers. He replied, "Mothers who see no wrong in their child. The teachers, authorities, others are always wrong, not their child."[13] He went on to say, "Sometimes parents seem to set their children up as 'gods' with almost a spirit of worship, seeing no wrong."[14]

The admonition to give a child praise and affirmation for what he is doing right, for the things he is doing well, for the good he is doing, must not be misconstrued as a signal to worship one's child. Rather, these verbal expressions of love are to let your child know you value him as a special gift to you from the Lord, a gift who must be encouraged in the ways of God. The idea is not to treat him as if he can do no wrong or to dish out continuous mindless flattery. It is giving your children genuine affirmation and commendation for praiseworthy deeds and behavior; and it is carrying out this exercise at the proper time, in the proper way.

Proverbs 3:27–28 says it best: "Do not withhold good from those to whom it is due, when it is in the power of your hand to do so. Do not say . . . 'Go, and come back, and tomorrow and I will give it,' when you have it with you" (NKJV). Don't wait until it's too late to tell your children you love them and are proud of them. "A word aptly spoken is like apples of gold in settings of silver" (Prov. 25:11 NIV).

Yes, if I could do it over,
I would praise my children more!

A child is fed with milk and praise.
MARY LAMB, *GOD'S LITTLE DEVOTIONAL BOOK FOR MOMS*

A happy childhood is one of the best gifts that
parents have it in their power to bestow.

MARY CHOLMONDELEY, *GOD'S LITTLE DEVOTIONAL BOOK FOR MOMS*

Chapter 2

I Was Too Serious

> A merry heart doeth
> good like a medicine.
> PROVERBS 17:22 KJV

Laughter is good medicine for us all. As someone once said, "There is no danger of developing eyestrain from looking on the bright side of things."[1] In the book *Tough-Minded Parenting*, the authors state: "Laughter is truly one of the most undervalued elements of life. Psychological research has clearly established laughter as an essential emotional nutrient in high levels of 'wellness.'"[2] Proverbs 15:15 tells us: "For the happy heart, life is a continual feast" (NLT).

As a preacher's kid (often called a P.K.), I learned early the value of laughing at myself, of not taking myself or the teasing I received too seriously. P.K.s have always been prime targets for jokes and kidding. To survive living in the "glass house" of a minister's family, preachers' kids have to learn to smile and shrug off the verbal barrage that often comes their way.

A Serious-Minded Family

Even though I personally learned that some things in life must not be taken too seriously, I do not think I adequately transferred this concept into my child raising. Life was serious business for my husband and me. I admit that we rarely "let our hair down" with our kids. We both came from fine Christian homes, but there wasn't a lot of "clowning around" in either of our families. It naturally followed that the atmosphere in the Maddox household was not too light-hearted either.

A Desire to Have Fun

The problem was *not* that we didn't want our family to have fun. Roland and I decided early in our marriage that we wanted to provide as many fun things as possible for our children. We made a genuine effort to incorporate into our schedule a variety of opportunities for entertainment and laughter. Nearly every year we took our children to the beach in Florida for a family vacation. There were two special trips to Disney World. We bought a ski boat when our kids were teenagers so we would have something fun to do together as a family. Every Fourth of July and Labor Day (if at all possible) were spent at a lake in Hot Springs, Arkansas, with dear friends and their families. We had a lot of great times of togetherness.

Yet as I reflect upon all those special times, I don't think we enjoyed them as fully as we could have; we didn't laugh enough on these "fun" adventures. I believe this was partly because I was often uptight—worrying about my children's behavior, their safety, their relationships, or other problems—both real and imagined. Not being very adept at playing, I became "the great protector." If I saw unhappy kids, I tried to rectify the situation. If I felt my children were not being as kind or as thoughtful as possible, I admonished them to be more loving. In some instances, I just worried about things in general. Those times when I did relax, everyone had more fun.

Looking back, I ask myself some questions: *Did I have unrealistic expectations? Was I trying to make my children act like little adults instead of the children they were? Was I afraid of what they might do or of what might happen to them? Did I want my children to behave perfectly in front of others?*

Wanted: A Fun Mom

Our kids did enjoy our vacations and our lake experiences; they will unquestionably agree with that assessment. Still, I believe we could have had more fun if I had been *a more fun mom.* I remember feeling guilty when I heard a pastor friend of mine describing his home. He said that they laughed a lot, joked a lot, and had a lot of fun as a family. That is what I wanted my children to say about our family—but I wasn't sure they could.

Wanted: A Fun Home

We didn't have serious illnesses. There was no divorce in our immediate families; our family was very stable. We didn't have great financial difficulties. We lived in a nice house, and our children attended good schools. We belonged to a wonderful church. We had so much for which to be thankful. Our home was a *happy* home, but was it a *fun* place to live?

What about your home? Is it a *fun* place to be?

21

William Makepeace Thackeray as quoted in *God's Little Devotional Book for Moms* said, "A good laugh is sunshine in the house."[3] Is your house full of sunshine and laughter? Do your children's friends *love* to come to your house? If I could go back in time, I would play more games with my children—whether I felt like it or not. I would laugh more with them. I would laugh more at my mistakes. I would "let my hair down" more. I would really *work* at playing with them. I would try to make times together more fun, more enjoyable.

Work at It

Perhaps this is not as big a problem for moms and dads today as it was for us. In the twenty-first century, much emphasis has been placed on togetherness and having fun as a family. But if you are by nature a serious person and you don't "let your hair down" as often as you'd like, my advice is this: *Working* at *playing* with your children is worth the effort.

As you look down the road to the future, what do you want your children to remember? That Mom was always fussing at them, not allowing them to act like the children they were? That Mom's unrealistic expectations made her too demanding because she was afraid of what others might think? Or that Mom took time to play and laugh with her family—that home was the most fun place on earth? We do not want our children to look back and think that growing up in their home was only existing, merely coping through a twenty-four-hour day. Patty Hankins, a minister's wife, says that life for the Christian is not meant to be "crisis living"—"breathlessly running

22

from one crisis to the next."[4] Rather, it is to be the abundant life of John 10:10: "I am come that they might have life, and that they might have it more abundantly" (KJV). And because God tells us that "a merry heart doeth good like a medicine" (Prov. 17:22 KJV), part of that abundant life surely includes a lot of laughter. St. Augustine once prayed: "O Holy Spirit, descend plentifully into my heart. Enlighten the dark corners of this neglected dwelling and scatter there Thy cheerful beams."[5]

Are You Uptight?

Being less serious-minded doesn't mean being a softy, a mom who doesn't discipline and train her children in the way they should go. I am a firm believer in discipline and proper training. It is also my fervent belief we should set definite boundaries for our children. However, is it not true that many of us parents are just too uptight? We don't relax enough and really enjoy those children God has given into our care. Ruth Ann VanderSteeg, mother of five adult children, reminds us: "We are in the building business. Builders are excited about what they are doing. Look forward to every stage of your child's life, from infancy to adulthood. Don't be so uptight, have fun with them."[6]

My friend Vicki Snider once spoke to a group of mothers of teenagers on the subject "Lighten up." She admonished us to "relax a little and have fun with our teens. That was good advice no matter our children's ages or stages. I wonder—do you need to "lighten up"?[7]

Christians Should Have the Most Fun

I believe it is vitally important not to give the impression (or even worse, cause our children to believe) that non-Christians have more fun than Christians. Christians should be the most fun people on earth because we, of all people, know the meaning of true happiness and real joy. Our lives should be filled with joy and laughter because we belong to Jesus Christ, the source of all happiness and joy. When a child is not having fun at home, isn't he more likely to seek out whoever *is* having fun? Kids want to have a good time. They are programmed that way. Stifling their childhood instincts and desires for fun is not the answer. As Eric Brand, businessman and father of four, said, "Kids learn to play *with* their parents or they learn to play *without* their parents."[8]

Let's Have Some Fun

I have asked several friends the following question: "What did *you* do (or observe other Christian families doing) to convey the idea that children from Christian families can have as much, or more fun than non-Christians?" I received some great replies. Veteran mom Ruth Ann VanderSteeg said, "Children of Christian families can have a lot of fun. The first thing to remember is, they are just children, and children like to have good times. Also remember that they have endless energy. Our family did things with a lot of activity that involved other Christian friends. We tried to do something special as a family once a week."[9]

Patty Hankins, one of the most fun moms I know, shared this timely advice: "Never stop an activity without replacing it with something that makes the change wonderful—something that doesn't make your children feel like all that's left is a boring void. Make out an exchange list just as you would when you are changing your diet to healthy eating. You merely exchange one activity for another. Ask God to lead you, through his creative power, to make this a positive experience, not a legalistic, negative approach. Also, remember that at first it will feel uncomfortable or odd—change always does."

Rob and Vicki Mullins, who have been in Christian ministry for many years and are currently serving at Bellevue Baptist Church in Cordova, Tennessee, answered the question in this way: "We just did it. We followed the Lord and he brought the fun. We ran with people who felt the same way. He can give you the creativity to make up for a 'forbidden' activity. We showed them [our children] the natural consequences of living away from the Lord and the benefits of walking with him. We never suffered. There were disagreements about what they could not do and what others could do, but we always lined our lives up with the Word of God. A favorite phrase was, 'Others may, but you cannot.'"[10]

Dr. Van Snider advised Christian parents to "get out in the world and play like crazy; keep your values, morals, and ideals so that you can be a 'light.' Get out in the church and play like crazy, showing your children the value of listening to the right leaders and hanging out with kids who share their values, and more importantly, their Savior."[11]

Enjoy, Enjoy, Enjoy!

As a mom whose children are grown I have some final words of advice: Our kids grow up and leave the nest all too soon, so let them be children. Don't try to make them little adults; you don't want them to grow up too fast. They need to enjoy the early years of their lives and be allowed to have fun. All too soon the pressing issues of adulthood will be upon them.

Parents, don't miss the joy of your child's growing up days! A child is a gift from God. Unwrap this special package and *enjoy, enjoy, enjoy!*

If I could start over, I would have more fun with my children!

The best way to keep children at home is to make home a pleasant atmosphere—and to let the air out of the tires.

DOROTHY PARKER, *GOD'S LITTLE DEVOTIONAL BOOK FOR MOMS*

In practicing the art of parenthood an ounce of
example is worth a ton of preachment.

WILFRED PETERSON, *GOD'S LITTLE DEVOTIONAL BOOK FOR MOMS*

Chapter 3

I "Preached" Too Much

> But speaking the truth in love, we are to grow up in all aspects into Him who is the head, even Christ.
>
> EPHESIANS 4:15 NASB

My husband has always accused me of being a third-generation preacher—following in the footsteps of my father and grandfather, both Southern Baptist ministers. But that was definitely not God's plan for my life as a woman. I am certain, however, that much of the *teaching* I directed toward my children did sound a whole lot like *preaching,* for I wanted so much to convey to them a strong sense of right and wrong and a thorough understanding of biblical principles.

Sermonizing

To me, everything was basically black or white; there were few gray areas. I might give a "sermon" on unchristian television programming or admonish my kids about choosing the right friends. Sometimes it was a soliloquy about diligence in schoolwork. It really did not take much for me to launch forth into sermonizing—I just wanted to be sure they knew where their daddy and I stood.

At times when I was aware that my "preaching" was having no effect, I devised other ways to teach important principles and values. One way was through "silent sermons." In our church one Sunday, an evangelist from Florida used a little saying in his sermon that I thought conveyed a powerful message. It went like this:

> Sin will take you further than you want to go.
>
> Sin will cost you more than you want to pay.
>
> Sin will keep you longer than you want to stay.[1]

I liked this adage so well that one night I decided to print it in sizeable black letters on a large sheet of white poster paper. After finishing the task, I carefully placed the poster against the wall at the bottom of the steps so my two teenagers would see it when they came down to breakfast the next morning. I still remember the moans and groans I heard when they first saw it at the foot of the steps. Their less-than-enthusiastic reception did not prompt me to move it from its prominent viewing place. I left it there for several days, hoping it was making at least a tiny impression. A few months later our son came home from school and told me he had heard those exact words in a chapel service at his Christian school. I knew then that the poster had had an effect—he was familiar enough with the words to recognize them once more.

Many years later, when both of our adult children were members of the same church in Georgia, one of them called to tell me about their Sunday night service. A visiting minister was preaching that evening, and my children happened to be sitting together.

When the minister began his message, he announced that he was basing his sermon on the following adage:

Sin will take you further than you want to go.

Sin will keep you longer than you want to stay.

Sin will cost you more than you want to pay.

My kids looked at each other, closed their notebooks, and one said to the other, "We already know about this, don't we!" I praised the Lord that he had used my unorthodox method to get through to their minds and hearts. Evidently that "silent sermon" had resonated with them both.

A Painful Lesson

As the years went by, I tried very hard not to sound so preachy in my motherly counsel. Sometimes God would stop me in my tracks to make me aware that I was "preaching" again. The greatest lesson I learned about my sermonizing came when my son was eighteen years old and a senior in high school. Although this lesson is not a pleasant memory, it is forever etched on my brain.

It was a typical weekday afternoon. Alan unlocked the front door, walked into the house, and headed for the kitchen where I was preparing dinner. We began to converse about his day at school. After talking for a few moments, he made a statement that really upset me. I began to "preach" an intense and pointed "sermon." It made him quite angry. He stormed out of the kitchen, up the stairs, and slammed shut the door to his room.

Immediately, I felt guilty. I knew I had "blown it" big time. Here I was, supposedly the mature Christian mother, and I had acted like an angry child. My preaching had gone from righteous indignation to simply venting my wrath. I was just plain angry!

I ran to my bedroom and, with great sadness, fell on my knees seeking God's forgiveness. I knew I must make things right with God before I could make them right with Alan. As I prayed, confessed my sins, and sought God's forgiveness, I opened my Bible to the book of James, chapter 1. Verse nineteen was very familiar and stood out immediately: "Everyone should be quick to listen, slow to speak and slow to become angry" (NIV). Then, as if it were in neon lights, verse 20 flashed before my eyes. If I had seen this verse before, it certainly had not attracted my attention as it did at that moment. James 1:20 states: "For the wrath of man does not produce the righteousness of God" (NKJV). The New International Version translates it this way: "For man's anger does not bring about the righteous life that God desires." As I read those words, I felt that God was clearly telling me that my angry, harsh words would not make my son godly—they would not produce the righteousness of God in his life. I must repent of my anger, asking God's forgiveness, as well as my son's. And one more thing God impressed upon my heart: I needed to stop preaching to this eighteen-year-old son of mine.

What a wake-up call! I could hardly wait to run upstairs and knock on Alan's door. Alan invited me to come in. For the next hour and a half, we had one of the best conversations we have ever had. I asked his forgiveness for my harsh and angry words.

After asking for his forgiveness, I shared with Alan that I knew I had been preaching to him for nearly eighteen years, but that day it was going to stop. I would begin the process of "letting go" and "letting God" have his way in my son's life. We agreed that by this time in his life he knew all the important biblical principles; he knew what his daddy and I believed; he

30

knew right from wrong. He had received Jesus Christ as his Savior and Lord as a young boy. Now, he was eighteen years old—a young adult. It was time for me to step back and let him be an adult—without my interference. I would continue to intercede daily—and sometimes hourly—on his behalf. I would be there for him when he needed me, but the time had come for my preaching to stop.

Times, Tones, Terms

Alan didn't hear as much preaching from his mom after that. I still have definite opinions which I do express. In these past few years, however, I have learned to couch them in less preachy terms. You see, I learned (though I still must be reminded from time to time) that there are three important T-words to remember when we parents are trying to get across our beliefs and ideas:

- Times
- Tones
- Terms

Times: We need to choose carefully the *times* we share our views and express our concerns. With girls, we can usually schedule a time to sit down with them and talk. With boys, we may have to catch them at a good time. During the teenage years it seemed that the best time for me to talk with my son was while I was cooking supper. He would often come and sit on the kitchen counter behind me. We seemed to communicate better that way than in a face-to-face confrontation. Timing is very important. Also remember: (1) if the child is hungry, feed him first, and (2) don't try to compete with his favorite TV show!

Tones: I must watch my *tone* of voice. Most of us have heard someone say, "Don't speak to me in that tone of voice." This is a sign that one's tone of voice is reflecting his emotional state. The tone of my voice may determine how the listener "hears" me—how he perceives what I am trying to say to him. If I have a conversation with a family member and my tone of voice is high pitched and loud, I may lose him or her right away, or receive a response I do not want to hear. When our ability to communicate is being adversely affected by our own negative emotions, we must stop and seek God's enablement in what we wish to convey. Only he can empower us in every situation to speak with grace.

Terms: Last of all, we need to make sure our *terms* are loving and kind—we are to speak the truth lovingly. Ephesians 4:15 says: "But speaking the truth in love, we are to grow up in all aspects into Him who is the head, even Christ" (NASB).

Speak the Truth in Love

Because I have always had the desire to speak truthfully—to be forthright in all I say—"speaking the truth *in love*" has been a constant challenge for me. A short trip from Brentwood, Tennessee, to Parsons, Tennessee, reminded me of the need to incorporate this verse into my life on a daily basis. Our seven-year-old granddaughter, Emily, was in the backseat of my car with her nine-year-old brother, Riley. They had been spending a few days with us at our home in Brentwood. I was taking them back to their mother. At one point during the trip, Riley did something that irritated me. I quickly scolded him.

Emily waited a moment or two and then she asked, "Grandmother, have you heard of the verse, *'speaking the truth in love'?*" I told her, "Yes." She then continued, "Grandmother, do you think you were speaking the truth in love?" I had to confess that I had not been. I asked forgiveness of both of my grand-children, praying that I would not forget that important little "sermon" from my precious granddaughter. Each of us must *speak the truth in love.*

Angry Monologues Produce Angry Dialogues

Although I admit to "preaching" to my children throughout the years they lived at home, I do not believe it is the best way for a mother to teach her children principles and values. This is especially true if the "sermon" turns into a monologue filled with anger. Angry monologues can bring on angrier dia-logues! The writer of Proverbs warned: "A soft answer turns away wrath, but a harsh word stirs up anger" (15:1 NKJV). If I could repeat my parenting years, my motto would be: "Speaking the truth in love" (Eph. 4:15 NASB).

Gracious Speech

We *are* to be firm in our convictions, but we must verbalize our values in a kind and loving way. We mothers are to speak as did the virtuous woman in Proverbs 31:26: "She opens her mouth in wisdom, and the teaching of kindness is on her tongue" (NASB). Our speech is to be "with grace, seasoned, as it were, with salt, so that you may know how you should respond to each person" (Col. 4:6 NASB).

A Meek and Quiet Spirit

As a young mother, I often heard teachings on 1 Peter 3:4, which reads: "a meek and quiet spirit, which is in the sight of God of great price" (KJV). The New King

33

James Version translates it in this way: "a gentle and quiet spirit, which is very precious in the sight of God." The desire to have a meek and quiet spirit was implanted in my heart, but I knew I wasn't meek and quiet by nature. Should I try to alter my personality? God showed me that the solution would be found not in attempting to change my personality but rather through examining my heart. *The Women's Study Bible* says, "This quality [of a meek and quiet spirit] is not a reference to genetically acquired personality traits, such as being a person of few words, but rather to an attitude marked by the absence of anxiety, coupled with a trust in God as the blessed controller of all things."[2] An attitude marked by the absence of anxiety: that is what God desired *for* me. Trust in the blessed controller of all things: that is what God desired *from* me.

Our heavenly Father wants our hearts to be right with him and our wills to be surrendered to his control. Our words may need to be strong, but they must come from a heart that is yielded to him. Only the Holy Spirit can work in us so that we will have a meek and quiet spirit. We must allow him to do so. *The Women's Study Bible* further states: "A woman characterized by a 'gentle and quiet' spirit is not only precious to God and a glory to her husband, but a joy to all who are around her."[3] Isn't that the way all of us women would like to be?

The Words of My Mouth— the Meditation of My Heart

The psalmist expressed for us what I believe should be our daily prayer: "May the words of my mouth and the meditation of my heart be pleasing in your sight,

O LORD, my Rock and my Redeemer" (Ps. 19:14 NIV). For my words to be pleasing in God's sight, the meditations of my heart must first be pleasing. If my heart is not right with God, my words will not be acceptable to him. Matthew 15:18 says: "The things that proceed out of the mouth come from the heart" (NASB). (There is an old saying that states it another way: "What's down in the well, comes up in the bucket.") Another familiar Bible verse is Proverbs 23:7: "For as he thinks in his heart, so is he" (NKJV). We cannot expect good words to come out of a heart that is not "thinking right"—a heart that is not in tune with the Lord.

Alone in God's Presence

How will the words of my mouth and the meditations of my heart be acceptable in God's sight? How will I be able to consistently speak the truth in love? It can only happen as I spend time daily in the presence of the Lord, seeking to get my heart right with him and seeking his wisdom, his will, and his ways of accomplishing his purposes for me and for my children. As a Christian mother, I have discovered that spending time with my Lord each day is a *necessity*— I can't do without it; my children can't do without it. (For more on prayer, see chapter 8, "I Constantly Prayed for My Children.")

As Patsy Clairmont so appropriately reminds us: "When mommy talks to Jesus, we're *all* a lot better off."[4]

If I had it to do over, I would talk to Jesus a whole lot more and preach to my children a whole lot less.

Love is spelled T-I-M-E.

Chapter 4

I Was Often Too Busy

> Be very careful, then, how you live—not as unwise but as wise, making the most of every opportunity, because the days are evil.
>
> EPHESIANS 5:15–16 NIV

Our mobile society has been described as a "rat race" or "traveling in the fast lane." We are abuzz with activity. If we are not moving our bodies or our automobiles, we think we must be doing something wrong! When my husband and I were raising our children in the seventies and eighties, life wasn't quite as hectic, but it was still easy to get too involved in activities and adventures.

A Busy Stay-at-Home Mom

I was a stay-at-home mom, but I was always a busy mom! I found that you do not have to work outside the home to live in the "fast lane." Yet one day, while traveling at breakneck speed down life's highway, I came to a screeching halt because of some wise words from a very wise woman—my mother.

Melanie was twenty-one months old at the time, and I was pregnant with our son. I was running from one activity to another. My projects and Bible studies were excellent, praiseworthy endeavors, and much of my other work was Christ oriented also. However, I was so busy trying to balance all those good things with being a good mother and wife that I was exhausted! (We all know about that Super Mom business!) Ironically, guess who was suffering the most—my family!

Amidst all this activity came Mother's words:

"Sarah, those activities you are engaged in will be there to go back to; those children *never* will. They will grow up and be gone before you know it."[1]

Her words stung! I knew my focus was not really on my children. In fact, it was everywhere else but at home. Something was not right. I realized that I must stop and do a major evaluation of my priorities. The Lord Jesus was first on my priority list, and my husband and my children came next—not my activities , projects, and committees. It was time to change my lifestyle accordingly.

A short time later when I was sharing my mother's words with a dear friend, this friend told me about a lady she saw while visiting her aunt at a nearby nursing home. Nearly every week, just inside the front door of the retirement home, this elderly woman was seated in a wheelchair. Always perfectly groomed and attired in a beautiful outfit, she seemed to be waiting to go somewhere special. Sadly, this lady was not really going anywhere; she just *thought* she was. In her state of dementia, she believed she was young again, living the active life of her past.

After my friend shared that story, I asked myself a probing question: *Will my children look back on their childhood and remember a mother who was always dressed up and going somewhere, doing 'important' work?* That was not the way I wanted to be remembered. Nothing was more important than raising my children. I needed to make sure nothing interfered with that awesome task!

A Change in Plans

For several years, I did slow down, and my priorities were in the right order. When my second child was in kindergarten, however, God had to get my attention again. By this time I was a small-group leader in a citywide Bible study in Memphis. It was a wonderful study. I loved being a group leader. The fellowship was marvelous, but it required two mornings a week plus a day of calling the women in my group. It was taking a lot of my time and energy.

For some reason, I did not pray much before taking this leadership role for a third year. I just assumed this was still God's plan for my life. (Mistake number one: don't ever assume something is God's plan for you—check it out with him first to be sure.) When August rolled around that year, I dutifully went to the first group leaders' meeting being held at a church in midtown Memphis. As I sat in the chapel of that beautiful church, all of a sudden a feeling of uncertainty came over me.

Am I not supposed to be doing this? I asked myself. *Is this not God's plan for me for this year?* I pondered. The longer I sat there, the more uncomfortable I became. I had no peace about being a group leader. I realized at that moment that I had not sought God's face—I had

38

not asked him if *his* plans for me included this Bible study assignment. As I sat there in misery, it dawned on me that this would be the last year my son would be in school for only a half day. He needed his mom's full attention every afternoon. My mother's words came back to me: *Those activities will be there to go back to; those children never will.* If I missed spending that time with Alan, I would never have the opportunity to make it up to him. I had not received God's permission and had made a mistake. I knew then that I must correct it. There was a problem, however. In this particular study the guidelines were firm: if you accepted a responsibility, you were expected to fulfill your commitment for the entire year.

My heart was heavy. I was in agony. How could I tell our Bible study teacher what I knew God was telling me? As I prayed, I realized I must humble myself and call her. That afternoon I reluctantly telephoned her. When I explained what had happened, she agreed that I should not be a leader and graciously allowed me to get out of leadership. Immediately I was flooded with peace—the peace God gives you when you are in the center of his will. I would stay at home with Alan, seeking to give him the attention he needed. He was definitely a higher priority than my ministry.

I missed being with those ladies that year. I missed that ministry. But I shall never regret the time I spent with my son. I would not have missed that privilege for anything! That citywide Bible study and those other good things were there to go back to; my son was never in school for just a half day again. Until his graduation from high school, he was in school all day long every weekday except for holidays and summer vacations. That year had been a God-appointed time for both of us.

Taking Care of Our Boys

Children desperately need our time and attention as they grow up. Dr. James Dobson, noted child psychologist and Christian leader, stated this principle well in *Bringing Up Boys*: "Boys are like automobiles that need a driver at the steering wheel every moment of the journey, gently turning a half inch here and a quarter inch there. They will need this guidance for at least sixteen or eighteen years, or even longer. When left to their own devices, they tend to drift toward the center divider or into the ditch, toward misbehavior or danger. Yet 59 percent of today's kids come home to an empty house. It is an invitation to mischief or disaster for rambunctious males, and the older they get, the more opportunities they have to get into trouble. Today, when the culture is in a tug-of-war with families for control of our children, we can't afford to be casual about their care and training."[2]

"God Doesn't Push, He Leads"

I wish I could state that as my children grew older, I was never again too busy, but that would not be the truth. Those years were filled with bustling activity. If I had it to do over, I would not fill my life with so much "going" and "doing." I would seek to lower my stress level for my own good and the good of my family. A friend of mine and fellow leader in our Bible study, Carolyn Campbell, once told me: "God doesn't push, He leads. If you feel 'pushed,' it is not God." What a timely admonition. I have since thoughtof her words of caution many times when

I felt "pushed." It was my desire to be *led* of the Lord, not to be *pushed* by my own or someone else's agenda.

When asked what she thought was one of the biggest mistakes today's mothers make, Ruth Ann VanderSteeg answered: "Selfishness in planning their lives around *their* plans rather than God's purpose for them. Failing to realize that in all of life there are seasons, and raising children is a season of life." Then she added: "The greatest opportunity I have ever had to please my Lord was raising my children to know and love him."[3] What a beautiful testimony!

An Evaluation

I cannot go back and live my life over, but I can advise mothers everywhere to periodically stop and evaluate their priorities, their activities, their schedule. Perhaps it would be beneficial to ask these questions: "Is the plan I am following during this season of my life God-ordained or self-ordained?" "Am I putting my family first or am I preoccupied with my own agenda or career?" "Am I allowing others (school and daycare) to raise my children?" "Am I permitting my children to be too busy with their activities?" "Have I consulted God before agreeing to do something, before accepting a position?"

Quality Time vs. Quantity Time

The age-old answer is often, "I am very busy, but I spend 'quality time' with my children." Is quality time really enough? It was interesting to read what George Barna had to say about quality time in his book *The Future of the American Family*: "There is no research that supports the view that the quality of the time parents and their offspring spend together is an acceptable substitute for the quantity of time committed to that relationship. Most studies have indicated that the quality-time/quantity-time debate is ill founded; the issue is not truly an 'either/or' choice, but a 'both/and' proposition. The children that grow up best adjusted and happiest in life are those whose parents spent considerable amounts of quality time with them."[4]

Statistics tell us that a century ago it was estimated that parents spent half their waking hours in activities which had to do with their children. In the late eighties, it was less than 20 percent.[5] I wonder what percentage of their waking hours parents will spend with their children in the twenty-first century?

Listen again to the wise words of Dr. James Dobson: "The harried lifestyle that characterizes most Westerners leads not only to the isolation of people from each other in the wider community, it is also the primary reason for the breakdown of the family. Husbands and wives have no time for each other, and many of them hardly know their children. They don't get together with relatives, friends, or neighbors because they are tyrannized by a never-ending 'to do' list. Repeatedly during my research in writing this book [*Bringing Up Boys*] . . . I came face-to-face with the same sad phenomenon. Parents were simply too distracted and exhausted to protect and care for their children."[6]

We dare not live such harried, busy lives! This is most assuredly *not* God's plan for the Christian family!

My counsel is to periodically

    STOP,

        LOOK,

            and LISTEN!

Stop what you are doing long enough to take a *look* at your life. Then really *listen* to what God is saying to you through his Word. In Psalm 46:10 God declares: "Be still, and know that I am God" (NIV). Stop for a while. Be still before God. In his daily devotional *A Psalm in My Heart,* Leroy Brownlow says: "This command [to be still] was not just for country folk who lived in a slow time and passive pace. Even today it is necessary to 'be still' to make progress."[7]

WHO'S IN CHARGE?

You and I are not in charge. God is. He is the Potter; we are the clay. He calls us aside to reflect upon this fact. He admonishes us: "Be still, and know that I am God." He calls us to stillness—to quietness and reflection so that we can know him better. Noted theologian John Phillips says: "We cannot know God if we are rushing here and there, with countless calls pulling us in various directions. We must learn to say an emphatic 'no' to some of the demands upon us. One of Satan's traps is to get us so involved in activity that we have no time to be still in the presence of God."[8]

This Scripture does not stop, however, with the admonition to "be still, and know that [he] is God." Psalm 46:10 goes on to echo God's resounding words: "I will be exalted among the nations, I will be exalted in the earth" (NIV). God wants to be exalted through our lives—in our very lifestyles. His plan is for us to live God-directed, not self-directed, lives; God-honoring, not self-honoring, lives. He wants to be Lord of our lives!

Stop . . . Be still . . . Write out all that you are doing. Then listen to his voice. Ask for his divine directions. "A man's heart plans his way, but the LORD directs his steps" (Prov. 16:9 NKJV). Pray about everything you believe you are to do. Evaluate your plans in the light of God's Word. (If need be, for more objectivity, enlist a family member or close friend to aid you in this task.) *Listen* to what God is saying to you about each activity, position, or project. "The plans of the heart belong to man, but the answer of the tongue is from the LORD" (Prov. 16:1 NASB). In Psalm 32:8 we are given a wonderful promise from our heavenly Father: "I will instruct you and teach you in the way you should go" (NIV).

Don't get ahead of the Lord; it is not a safe place to travel. Get his instructions first, then proceed with caution. *Stop, look,* and *listen* to the Lord. It's the only way to go!

> If I had it to do over,
> I would not be so busy!

> Discipline is loving your children to the max.
> DR. JAMES MERRITT

Chapter 5

I Didn't Discipline as Effectively as I Could Have

> Train up a child in the way he should go, even when he is old he will not depart from it.
>
> PROVERBS 22:6 NASB

Administering the appropriate discipline, effectively and consistently, was for me, as it is for most parents, a daunting task. If I could go back in time, I would certainly attempt to do a better job in the area of discipline. When our first child was born, the most popular book on child raising was Dr. Spock's famous handbook, *Baby and Child Care*.[1] Anyone familiar with the book knows of its permissive philosophy, which I believe proved detrimental to the welfare of many. I knew I did not want to apply this permissive philosophy to our children.

As the years progressed, God raised up Dr. James Dobson as the leading authority on raising godly children. Countless millions have been positively impacted by his expertise and insights. I shall never forget one weekend when my parents came to see us. By this time our children were school age. On Friday afternoon, Mother handed me a copy of Dr. Dobson's new book, *Dare to Discipline.* On Saturday, not knowing that Mother had brought me a copy, Daddy came into the kitchen with another copy of the same book. You can imagine that I got their message loud and clear: they obviously thought I really needed some help in the area of discipline!

Compliant or Strong-Willed

Our first child was compliant. She was very responsive to authority. I thought I was a pretty good disciplinarian—until along came the challenge of a strong-willed child. While it was not very comforting to read the following words from Dr. Dobson's excellent book *The Strong-Willed Child,* at least it assured my husband and me that we were not the only ones who might face such circumstances: "Just as surely as some children are naturally compliant, there are others who seem to be defiant upon exit from the womb. . . . As the months unfold, their expression of willfulness becomes even more apparent, the winds reaching hurricane force during toddlerhood."[2]

Many of us are *blessed* with strong-willed children. Perhaps you have one or you may have been one yourself. And yes, it is a blessing! Sometimes we may think it is a blessing in disguise, but it is a blessing. We learn much that we never would have learned in any other way.

How do you know if your child is strong-willed? I can assure you, it won't take you long to discover this fact. I remember what a pediatrician told a friend after evaluating her two-year-old child. He said, "Most two-year-olds come into a room questioning what they are going to do. Strong-willed children come into a room, decide immediately what they are going to do, and start to do it unless you stop them."[3]

Over the years I learned a lot about being the mother of a strong-willed child. For example, don't be surprised if you seem to be constantly correcting and restraining these children. Because you feel a need to watch them closely—trying to keep them out of trouble, etc.—if you are not careful, overcorrecting and overdirecting them will become a habitual practice. This may cause the child to feel he cannot do anything right. A wounded spirit may result, as well as the development of a poor self-image.

A timely admonition on which I often reflected was also found in *The Strong-Willed Child.* Dr. Dobson clearly pointed out the importance of shaping the will of the child while he is young. Then he added: "Our objective is not only to shape the will of the child . . . but to do so without breaking his spirit."[4] It was my job to shape my child's will, but in doing so I must be careful not to wound his spirit. What a difficult assignment!

To help parents facing this daunting task, Dr. Dobson offered six broad guidelines for shaping the child's will:

1. Define the boundaries before they are enforced.

2. When defiantly challenged, respond with confident decisiveness.

3. Distinguish between willful defiance and childish irresponsibility.

4. Reassure and teach after the confrontation is over.

5. Avoid impossible demands.
6. Let love be your guide![5]

Finding a Balance in Our Discipline

Whether we are the parents of a strong-willed child, a compliant child, or both, it is so essential to attempt to find the proper balance in our discipline. We must not be unduly hard on our children, but we must not be slack in our discipline either. What a monumental challenge!

In his latest book, *Bringing Up Boys,* Dr. Dobson gives this thought-provoking assessment:

[The] balance between compassion and judgment appears from Genesis to Revelation. It moves between Creation and the Fall, between condemnation and forgiveness, between the Crucifixion and the Resurrection, between heaven and hell. . . . Learning to balance the intersection between these two forces is especially useful to the understanding of children. There's a time for affirmation, tenderness, and love. They nourish the spirit and seal the bond between generations. But there's also a time for discipline and punishment. Moms and dads who try to be eternally positive, ignoring irresponsibility or defiance in their children, fail to teach them that behavior has consequences. But beware! Parents who are continually punitive and accusatory can create serious behavioral and emotional problems.[6]

The apostle Paul gave this warning to dads: "Fathers, do not provoke your children to anger, but bring them up in the discipline and instruction of the Lord" (Eph. 6:4 NASB). Only God can give us the wisdom, the grace, and the strength to find the proper balance in disciplining our children. To try and do so on our own would be an impossible task and a foolish endeavor.

Defining Discipline

What does it mean to *discipline* one's child? One dictionary definition is: "training to act in accordance with rules; instruction and exercise designed to train to proper conduct and action; to correct; to chastise."[7]

Mark Lee, in *Our Children Are Our Best Friends,* had this to say about discipline: "Discipline is not merely a punishing device but one for correction and training to guide future action. . . . Sincere love, explanation in the appropriate tone of voice, fairness, consistency and a score of other factors are involved. . . . Listening, guidance and follow-through are all important in discipline. And in all the business before us, we should be seeking to develop self-discipline in our children."[8]

Signposts on the Pathway to Effective Discipline

During the years our kids were growing up in our home, my husband and I found that God placed some signposts along our path to help us be more effective disciplinarians. I believe these are significant markers on the road to effective discipline. These seven signposts are:

1. Authority
2. Time
3. Training

4. Consistency
5. Consequences
6. Styles and Methods
7. Love

Authority

The first signpost parents must incorporate into their mindset concerning discipline is *authority*. It is important to establish who's in charge early in the child's life. The Bible clearly states: "Children, obey your parents in the Lord, for this is right" (Eph. 6:1 NASB). Parents are to be the authority in the home, not the opposite. We parents must be certain, however, that we do not misuse or abuse this God-given authority. Dr. Bill Slonecker, author of *Parenting Principles from the Heart of a Pediatrician,* said, "The message the child learns about authority when he is young will have a dramatic effect upon his understanding of God's authority later in life."[9]

To have authority *over* someone, we must first learn to be *under* authority—under God's authority and the authority of those he has placed over us. Therefore, as parents, if we expect our children to obey us and learn to submit to God's will in *their* lives, we must first learn to submit to God's authority and walk in obedience to his will in *our* lives. There is a lot of truth in the saying: "There are no undisciplined children; there are just undisciplined parents."[10] One famous mother had this to say about the fact that her two daughters had rebelled against authority and appeared to be undisciplined: "I just wanted them to be happy." The truth this mother and all parents must recognize is that an undisciplined, rebellious child is *not* happy. If we truly want our children to be happy,

50

then one of our primary goals as parents should be to teach our children submission to our authority and to God's.

Time

The second signpost God would have us utilize is *time*. I cannot overemphasize the importance of taking the time necessary to effectively discipline. You and I can try to take shortcuts, but it just won't work. Appropriate, effective discipline demands our time. Dr. Mark Lee says, "Discipline requires effort, and there is no labor-saving device available as a substitute for it."[11] Follow-through to see that the child submits to your authority will be time consuming, but it will surely be worth your effort.

The failure to follow through once an instruction or command is given seems to be a common practice among parents of all ages. I know it was a problem for me. As I have conversed with other moms through the years, I have found that I had a lot of company in this area. Often we do not follow through because we get busy doing something else.

Consider the following scenario that occurs in many homes: The mother tells her child to clean up his room. About an hour later she comes back to the room and nothing has been done. Of course, she gets upset and likely begins a small tirade. The child starts to pick up some of his things. She leaves the room again. In a few minutes she returns. Very little has been done. More fussing. More frustration. Perhaps a spanking or a scolding or a time-out. The entire experience is most unpleasant for parent and child, and very little has been accomplished.

What should the mother have done? I don't have all the answers, but if I could go back to those days, there is one thing I would change in my own parenting. When my children were preschoolers, I would have cut back on many of my own outside activities, allowing much more time to train my children to obey. I needed to be available to follow through *every time* I asked my child to do something—*to see to it that what I had asked him or her to do was carried out.* If I had done that, I believe there would have been less fussing, less frustration, and more time for fun. *Effective discipline takes time!*

Training

A third signpost for parents is *training.* Proverbs 22:6 says "Train up a child in the way he should go" (KJV). It is important to note that this verse does not say "teach a child . . ." Training incorporates teaching, but goes far beyond it. To *teach* means to "impart knowledge" or "to give instruction in."[12] To *train* means "to develop or form the habits, thoughts or behavior [of a person] by discipline and instruction."[13] Look at the difference in these two words. Over and over I can tell *(teach)* my child what I want done; but if I don't see him developing or forming the habits, thoughts, and behaviors toward which I am working, he may not really be "getting the message" of my teaching. His understanding of what is expected of him will come when I *train* him in the way he should go—when I help him develop and form the proper habits, thoughts, and behaviors through careful instruction *and* proper discipline. This training will only come if I take the time to follow through and be consistent in my discipline.

Consistency

Signpost number four is *consistency.* One reason I did not rebel as a preacher's kid was because of the consistency of my parents. They were consistent in their living; they were consistent in their discipline. I knew what was expected of me. I knew what the consequences would be if I did not obey. Consistency and follow-through are vitally important in raising a child. Dr. Charles Thompson, professor of educational psychology and counseling at the University of Tennessee in Knoxville, has said: "Kids find security in limits and consistency. If they can get away with something one day but they're punished for it the next, they don't know where the boundaries are."[14] Whether the child is strong-willed or not, he must know that when his parents tell him to do something, they mean it—not just this time, but every time. If he does not obey, there will be consequences.

Consequences

Closely tied to consistency is signpost five: *consequences.* An absolutely essential principle to teach our children early on is that sin has consequences. Galatians 6:7–8 says: "Do not be deceived: God cannot be mocked. A man reaps what he sows. The one who sows to please his sinful nature, from that nature will reap destruction; the one who sows to please the Spirit, from the Spirit will reap eternal life" (NIV). Our children need to know that behavior and consequences are connected—every wrong action has a consequence. What we sow we shall reap. They also need to be taught the "Law of the Harvest": We reap more than we sow, and we reap later than we sow.[15]

Peggy Perkins, former elementary school principal and former children's director was asked what advice she would give to new parents. She stated:

1. Love your children unconditionally, but establish limits and stick to them.

2. Don't be afraid to say no—you don't need to earn your child's approval.

3. Remain the parent in control, not your children's "buddy."

4. Make consequences fit the "crime"—and then stick to them; don't be talked into giving in.

5. Be unified in your philosophy of discipline.

6. Use God's Word—not as a club but as the ultimate authority in establishing limits and expectations for their behavior.[16]

Styles and Methods

The sixth signpost of discipline deals with *styles* and *methods*. If I could go back in time, I would make a careful study of each child's personality and then determine which method of discipline would be best for each. I think my husband and I sometimes erred by trying to discipline each child in the same manner. While one might require very little correction before he or she would respond in a certain situation, the other might require several forms of discipline for the desired effect in the same situation. Disciplining them in a similar manner did not always work.

An evaluation of one's style of discipline is a beneficial exercise. Dr. Ed Young, a pastor in Houston, Texas, was speaking on parenting on his radio program, *The Winning Walk*. He stated that there are four types of discipline styles parents use:

1. Autocratic
2. Permissive
3. Indifferent
4. Relational

He pointed out that the relational style of discipline is the best. Then he gave the following principle for all of us to remember: "Rules without relationship equal rebellion."[17] Many good books have been written on discipline styles. A careful perusal is a must for all parents. To be the most effective, we need to understand all we can about these styles and methods of discipline.

Love

Signpost number seven is *love.* We discipline our children because we love them. There are three underlying principles a child needs to know when he has been disciplined:

1. It was *not* done in anger.
2. It was *for his benefit.*
3. He was disciplined *because his parent loved him* too much to let him get away with the wrong behavior or action.

We are not to discipline in anger. All of our discipline is to be loving discipline. Dr. James Merritt, senior pastor of Cross Pointe, The Church at Gwinnett Center, in Duluth, Georgia, states: "Discipline is loving your children to the max."[18] We can look to God as our example. God loves *us* "to the max," and he disciplines us because he loves us. Hebrews 12:5 says: "My son, do not make light of the Lord's discipline, and do not lose heart when he rebukes you, because the Lord disciplines those he loves, and he punishes everyone he accepts as a son" (NIV).

In her book *Blended Families* Maxine Marsolini states: "Discipline is an act of love, not an opportunity to vent frustration and impose suffering. It is a loving means to train, prepare and mold a child. . . . Until discipline is meted out in love, it will have limited effectiveness and the potential to produce rebellion rather than positive change."[19]

Our heavenly Father disciplines us because he loves us. He disciplines us for our good. Likewise, we earthly parents are to discipline our children for their good. It won't be pleasant at the time, but it must be lovingly administered with the heartfelt desire that it will "produce a harvest of righteousness and peace" in our children's lives. Hebrews 12:9–11 states: "Moreover, we have all had human fathers who disciplined us and we respected them for it. How much more should we submit to the Father of our spirits and live! Our fathers disciplined us for a little while as they thought best; but God disciplines us for our good, that we may share in his holiness. No discipline seems pleasant at the time, but painful. Later on, however, it produces a harvest of righteousness and peace for those who have been trained by it" (NIV).

If I could go back in time, each time I disciplined my children I would hug them, assuring them of my love. (I'm certain that I often did this, but not as consistently as I should have done it.) Then I would pray with them, asking God to help them in their particular problem area. Our discipline must be *loving* discipline.

Banners Along the Way

In addition to the signposts God set on the pathway of my life, there were some "banners" that caught my attention. One I'll always remember asked: "Is it 'a high enough hill to die on'?" I first heard this verbalized when I was attending a women's meeting at our church. The speaker was Daisy Hepburn, an author and speaker from California. In her message to us she advised, before you "go to war" over an issue with your children (or your husband), be certain that it is "a high enough hill to die on."[20] That advice really stuck with me and the others who heard it. I realized that day that there were certain issues in the life of one of my children that were not "high enough hills to die on," and I had been treating them as if they were. Realizing this helped me turn my focus on what really mattered in my child's life—what would affect him in the future and for eternity. It made a difference in my response to his behavior.

There was another "banner" that was even more essential. It proclaimed the father's importance in the discipline of children. Looking back to my children's teenage days, I wish I had pulled back and allowed my husband to do more of the disciplining of our teenage son. Why? First, because my husband tends to view the entire picture, not just react to the crisis of the moment. Second, his personality is much more phlegmatic, and he handles situations carefully, deliberately, and thoughtfully. Third, I have come to believe that a teenage boy is much more open to his father's dealings with him (male to male) than he is to his mother's (female to male.) Our son, Alan, responded more readily to the words of his father. His daddy was a wonderful role model, and I wanted Alan to follow his dad's example. We were training our son to be the head of his home—the spiritual leader of his family. As Alan grew older, he needed even more opportunity to relate to his father. In a family, the father is important in the lives of his children—perhaps never more so than in the life of a teenage boy. The father is vital in the effective discipline of his children.

Dr. Van Snider was asked this question "What do you believe is the secret to effective discipline?" In reply he gave this formula:

1. *Fairness*—always the same. No need to show anger.

2. *Firmness*—no compromise. Concept of absolute truth.

3. *Finality*—(consistency). Same punishment for same misbehavior *every time*.[21]

If I could do it over, I would seek to
discipline my children more effectively.

---

section two

five things i did right

When Mother Teresa received her Nobel Prize, she was asked, "What can we do to promote world peace?" She replied, "Go home and love your family."

GOD'S LITTLE DEVOTIONAL BOOK FOR MOMS

Chapter 6

I Loved My Children and Their Daddy

> That they [the older women] may encourage the young women to love their husbands, to love their children.
>
> TITUS 2:4 NASB

A year and a half after Roland and I married, our first child, Melanie, made her entrance into our world. I was totally unprepared for what was to come. I had never fed a baby a bottle nor changed a diaper. I had never done much babysitting. There were no babies in our family or neighborhood to provide those experiences. I was a first-class greenhorn! I felt a lot like author Anne Tyler, who was quoted in *God's Little Devotional Book for Moms*, "I remember leaving the hospital . . . thinking, *Wait, are they going to let me just walk off with him? I don't know beans about babies!*"[1]

When I got home with Melanie, she had colic, which continued for six months. Added to that frustration was the fact that she developed a respiratory infection when she was only a week old. For the first four years of her life she was sick nearly every other week. Our son, Alan, came along when Melanie was two and a half years old. He also had colic, but not for as long.

I had very much wanted to be a mother, but I was totally baffled at what to do with sick and colicky children. To make things worse, no one seemed to have the solution to these problems. "What should I do?" was my frequent question. With the help of a loving heavenly Father, a wonderful husband, and two sets of long-suffering grandparents, we made it through those difficult years. I learned a great deal. Although it would take too many pages to enumerate all God taught me, please permit me to share a few of my insights—or hindsights (with a little humor thrown in for good measure).

Insights and Hindsights

1. It is necessary for a mother to give huge daily doses of love to her children, but it is not necessary for her to have a lot of sleep. I averaged only five hours of sleep a night for more than four years. As Shannon Fife, another sleep-deprived mom, states: "Insomnia [could be described as] a contagious disease often transmitted from babies to parents."[2]

2. There is no one answer to colic that I have ever found. Taking the baby riding in the car, swinging her in a baby swing, letting her sit in her infant seat next to a running clothes dryer, laying her on her tummy on mommy's knees, or giving colic drops may all work for some, but sometimes nothing works. You just have to love the baby and pray, pray, pray.

One night our baby daughter was awake all night long. She cried and I cried. I prayed, and she kept on crying. I did not want to disturb Roland, so she and I stayed as far away from the bedroom as was possible in our small apartment. I walked the floor with her, rocked her, laid her on her tummy on my lap, put her in her swing—all to no avail. Finally, about five o'clock in the morning, I was ready to "throw in the towel." Instead, I threw a cloth diaper across the room and then I woke up my husband. In my great frustration and exhaustion, I declared, "You have got to help me with this child! She has been awake all night!" I shall never forget what happened after that. He very calmly and lovingly took her from my arms, placed her beside him in the crook of his arm, and she immediately went to sleep. Needless to say, she has always been Daddy's Girl.

Just remember, the colicky stage will pass before you know it (but giving money for research into finding a cure for colic might also help).

3. One of the best ways to demonstrate your love to a sick child is through focused attention. Children want your focused attention when they are sick. They want your "all hereness," not your "all thereness." (I read that in a book somewhere.) One night I was sitting at the foot of Melanie's bed. I was not "all here"; my mind was miles away. She caught me at it, and I was embarrassed. I realized that night the importance of giving her my full attention. It is not enough just to be in the room with our children. As much as possible, we must give them our focused attention. That communicates true love.

4. Childhood illnesses may be traumatic and frustrating, but you can always look around and see

someone else's child who is much worse off. Our children overcame their illnesses and moved on to healthy lives. Some children never do. Others are born with handicaps that they and their parents must deal with all their lives. Be thankful if you have a "most of the time" healthy child. If you have a very sick child, God should be praised in this situation too. God is good all the time. He knows just what you need. He will never give you more than you can bear. Receive the children God gives you. Love them with all your heart. He always gives us what is best. And as you go to your heavenly Father in prayer, he will provide the grace and strength you need to care for your child, no matter how great may be his or her needs.

5. I discovered I could not love my children as I should unless I fully depended on my heavenly Father. Throughout my children's growing up years God taught me valuable lessons about love. My children were so dependent on me during that time I sometimes got tired of trying to meet their needs. But my God never tired of meeting *my* needs—and how very much I needed him! He didn't want me to seek to make it on my own, and I learned quickly that I could not. I had to look to the Lord. I desperately needed his daily and hourly help. I could not love my children or my husband as I should if I was not walking with his enablement. I could not make it on my own, in my own strength. When I neglected to come to him, he would draw me back to himself—through whatever means it took to get my attention.

A Never-to-Be Forgotten Lesson

Near the end of these difficult preschool years, God really spoke to me in a way I shall never forget. Because

I had attempted to take care of sickly, colicky babies and keep up with everything else I wanted to do, once again my priorities got out of whack. This time I found myself not only physically exhausted from so little sleep, but also emotionally drained and mentally whipped. And, although I did not realize it, I was spiritually depleted. All this "came home to roost" the morning after Dr. Martin Luther King, Jr. was killed in Memphis, Tennessee, in April 1968. Although it was a long time ago, it is a morning I shall always remember.

My children were at home with the housekeeper. The stay-at-home moms on our block had gathered at a neighbor's house for coffee to discuss the terrible events that had taken place in our city the day before. For about an hour we shared about the distressing times in which we lived. I must have been especially vocal, because all at once a neighbor turned to me and exclaimed: "Sarah, for a Christian, you sure are miserable!" Those words were like a dagger piercing my heart. I could not believe what my ears had heard. As quickly as I could, I excused myself, ran out of the neighbor's house, and hurried back to mine. When I was safely inside, I dashed up the steps, shut my daughter's bedroom door, and fell to my knees.

Wouldn't you know that just the week before, my mother had sent me a wonderful new book—*Go Home and Tell,* by Miss Bertha Smith, missionary to China. Obviously, this was God's perfect timing for me. I had only gotten to read a few pages in the book, but at that moment I remembered something Miss Bertha had suggested. She advised that any time you come to a crossroads in your life, knowing something has to change, take an inward look. On your knees before the

Lord, with pen and paper, list everything in your life that you know is not right. Confess each sin to God and ask his forgiveness. First John 1:9 says: "If we confess our sins, He is faithful and righteous to forgive us our sins and to cleanse us from all unrighteousness" (NASB). Then she suggested: "When all sins that can be recalled are listed, it is good to pray the following prayer: 'Lord, You are light. Shine into my heart and show me anything which should not be there.'"[3] It reminded me of the prayer that the psalmist prayed: "Search me, O God, and know my heart; test me and know my anxious thoughts. See if there is any offensive way in me" (Ps. 139:23–24 NIV).

For the next few hours I followed her advice. I spent that time in confession, asking for God's forgiveness and cleansing. It was one of the most painful, and yet most freeing, experiences I have ever had.

But the process was not to end there. Miss Bertha had gone on to share that after we have followed her suggested procedure and have received God's forgiveness and cleansing, we must dethrone "self" and enthrone Jesus Christ, asking him to fill us with his Holy Spirit. This had to be done, she said, "by a definite act of my will and of faith."[4] I spent the next few moments seeking to follow this godly admonition.

I then disposed of my list of forgiven sins by tearing it into tiny pieces. (Today I would shred it in an electric shredder.) This significant act was a symbolic way of reminding me that my sins had been forgiven—no longer to be remembered by a loving heavenly Father.

As I walked down the stairs of my home, I felt the greatest peace I had felt in years. God had gotten my attention that day so that he could reveal to me what was wrong in my life. He clearly showed me that my basic problem was not physical, emotional, or mental—it was a spiritual problem. He showed me that during this difficult time of my life, I had failed to deal with some negative emotions that had emerged and had subsequently been submerged. I also came to see that I had put everything else ahead of spending time with the Lord. I had left very little time for him. "Self" was on the throne of my life. Sadly to say, my love for Jesus had grown cold.

That was a long, long time ago. Since that day, whenever I find myself starting on a downward spiral—when I'm exhausted, overwhelmed, discouraged— I take an inward look. I ask God to reveal to me if there is any unconfessed sin within my heart. If he reveals something to me, I confess and forsake it, asking for God's forgiveness and cleansing. Then I ask him to "create in me a pure heart, O God, and renew a steadfast spirit within me. . . . Restore to me the joy of your salvation" (Ps. 51:10, 12 NIV). What a freeing experience it always is. I have found that it is the only way to live! It's the only way to love!

I cannot live a victorious Christian life on last week's spiritual food any more than I can eat once a week or once a month and expect to function physically and mentally. No matter my age or stage, Jesus Christ is to have first priority in my life. If he does not, everything else will suffer—my own life and certainly the lives of my family members. If I do not spend time alone with God, I will not be filled with his love. If I am not filled with his love, I will not be able to love my family in the way I should. You and I can have a deep desire to truly love our children. But if we are not truly loving the Lord and allowing him to pour his love into us, his love—the love they need so desperately—cannot flow out of us to them. There must be an in-flow to have an out-flow.

Agape Love

God's love is *agape* love. It is unconditional love—love that is given regardless of the worthiness of the recipient. This is the kind of love we are to give our children. It is clearly delineated in the thirteenth chapter of 1 Corinthians. A portion of this chapter states: "Love suffers long and is kind; love does not envy; love does not parade itself, is not puffed up; does not behave rudely, does not seek its own, is not provoked, thinks no evil; does not rejoice in iniquity, but rejoices in the truth; bears all things, believes all things, hopes all things, endures all things. Love never fails" (vv. 4–8 NKJV).

While I was reading 1 Corinthians 13 one day, I took out my notebook and wrote:

Love endures all things
the sleepless nights
the stinky diapers
the spit-up
the first fall
the potty training
the mounds of dirty clothes
the terrible twos
the barrage of "no's"
the annual birthday parties
the pouting and crying
the first neighborhood fight
the never-ending sports events
the emotional upheavals
the rebellious teenagers

Love is patient
with the baby who's sickly and colicky
with the faltering attempts to take that
first step
with the slow talker
with the tiresome process of learning to
tie shoes
with the discordant sounds of musical
instruments
Love is kind
to the child who messes up
to the child who can't hit the ball or
catch it either
to the child who isn't like me
to the child who doesn't understand
to the child who is handicapped
to the child who is mentally challenged
Love does not behave rudely
when my child embarrasses his family
when my child misbehaves
when my child disobeys
when my child acts unseemly
Love is not easily provoked
by the child who is slow
by the child who asks a million questions
by the child who interrupts
by the child who continually messes up
by the child who spills his milk
by the child who ruins my "treasures"
Love is not puffed up
when her child wins and her friend's
child loses
about her child's talents or successes

  Love does not promote her child above others
or seek the best place for her child
  Love is not envious of a friend's child who
is prettier, smarter, and more likable than
hers
  Love does not rejoice when a friend's child
falls, but rejoices when that child "walk[s] in
the truth" (3 John 4 NKJV).
  Love does not give up on her rebellious and
wayward child
  Love
"bears all things,
believes all things,
hopes all things,
endures all things"
because she trusts in her Lord with all her
heart, leaning not on her own understanding (see Prov. 3:5).
  Morning, noon, and night
she cries out to God
in earnest intercession
for this precious child she loves so much.
  "And now abide faith, hope, love, these
three; but the greatest of these is love"
(1 Cor. 13:13 NKJV).

That morning, in a new and poignant way, God
reminded me of how important it is for me to love
my child with the love of the Lord! That is possible
only through his power, with his grace, as I am filled
with his Holy Spirit. I am totally dependent on him.
Major Ian Thomas once admonished us to pray in
this way, saying: "Lord, I cannot; You never said
I could. You can. You always said You would."[5] "I can

do everything through him who gives me strength" (Phil. 4:13 NIV).

Love the Child, Love His Father

As essential as it was for my children to know that I loved *them,* it was of the utmost importance to me for them to know that I loved their *dad.* Experts often tell us that the best way a mother can make her children feel loved is to love their father. Dr. Van Snider wrote: To make a child feel loved, "parents first must love one another openly so that children see tender acts and hear tender words."[6] My husband, Roland, and I wanted our children to have no doubts about their mother and daddy's love and commitment to each other. We sought to clearly convey that message to them day after day. As soon as they were old enough, we told them the story of our courtship—of how God had led us to each other as soulmates. (On our second date, Roland told me he was going to marry me. A year and a half later, he did.)

Love for a Lifetime

I praise God for giving me a fantastic Christian husband who has devotedly loved and cared for me year after year. On that day in June 1962 when Roland and I pledged our fervent love and lifetime commitment to our marriage, we entered into a covenant with God and with each other. Divorce was not—and never will be—an option. We made that fact very clear to our children. They knew their daddy was *never* going to leave their mother, and their mother was *never* going to leave their daddy. It was our sincere desire that they grow up secure in that knowledge.

What the Bible Teaches about Marriage, Family, and Sexuality

Not only did we seek to model before our children the biblical example of marriage, but also to pass down to them a clear understanding of what God's Word teaches about marriage and the family. We wanted to prepare them as much as possible for their own marriages.

Marriage. The Bible clearly and unequivocally teaches that a "marriage" is one man and one woman joined together for a lifetime in a covenant with each other and with God. God's plan for marriage is introduced in the second chapter of Genesis and repeated in the New Testament in Matthew 19 and Ephesians 5. Genesis 2:24 states: "Therefore a man shall leave his father and mother and be joined to his wife, and they shall become one flesh" (NKJV). Matthew 19:4–6 says: "'Have you not read that He who made them at the beginning made them male and female,' and said, 'For this reason a man shall leave his father and mother and be joined to his wife, and the two shall become one flesh'? 'So then, they are no longer two but one flesh. Therefore what God has joined together, let not man separate'" (NKJV). In God's sight marriage is a lifetime commitment to one's mate and to the Master, the Lord Jesus. It is a covenant—a permanent agreement—not to be severed for as long as the husband and wife live.

Spouses are to "cleave" to each other (Gen. 2:24 KJV). God hates divorce. Malachi 2:16 says this explicitly: "'I hate divorce,' says the LORD, the God of Israel" (NASB). Trials in marriage are inevitable, but our God is able—able to make a way where there seems to be no way, "able to do exceedingly abundantly above all that we ask or think, according to the power that works in us" (Eph. 3:20 NKJV). As Dr. Adrian Rogers once said: "When you get on the matrimonial airplane, throw away your parachute."[7]

Family and sexuality. My husband and I taught our children that a "family" is a group of people who are related to each other by marriage, by birth, or by adoption. Homosexuality is described in God's Holy Word as "shameful" (Rom. 1:27 NKJV) and "an abomination" (Lev. 18:22 NKJV). In Mark 10:6, Jesus declared: "But at the beginning of creation God 'made them male and female'" (NIV). Establishing in our children's minds a clear picture of maleness and femaleness was crucial to their emotional and spiritual development.

Sexual purity. With verses such as Ephesians 5:3, Colossians 3:5, and 1 Thessalonians 4:3, we tried to instill in our kids a basic understanding that premarital sex, adultery, sex outside of marriage, and abortion is wrong. Foundational to these teachings are the verses in 1 Corinthians that say: "Or do you not know that your body is the temple of the Holy Spirit who is in you, whom you have from God, and you are not your own? For you were bought at a price; therefore glorify God in your body and in your spirit, which are God's" (6:19–20 NKJV). God says in 1 Peter 1:16: "'Be holy, for I am holy'" (NKJV). Our teachings embraced the need to continually examine our own hearts and deal regularly with any sins in our own lives. Each of us needs to heed the admonition of the apostle Paul in Colossians 3:5–6: "Put to death, therefore, whatever belongs to your earthly nature: sexual immorality, impurity, lust, evil desires and greed, which is idolatry" (NIV). Then we must follow Paul's challenge in verses 1 and 2 of this same chapter: "Since, then, you have been raised with Christ, set your hearts on things above, where Christ is seated at the right hand of God. Set your minds on things above, not on earthly things."

Our family was what is today designated a *nuclear family*—mother, father, and children all living under the same roof. Sadly, no longer is the nuclear family the norm in America. More and more families, both Christian and non-Christian, have been affected by separation and divorce. Our purpose has not been to condemn those who have experienced divorce, but to do everything possible to strengthen marriages. Many times we have asked ourselves and others: What can be done to reverse this onslaught of divorces, even among Christian families? What can we do to assure that our children have a biblical worldview of marriage and family?

I believe senior adults—older men and women—need to follow the admonition found in the second chapter of Titus. We older women need to teach and train the younger women "to love their husbands and children, to be self-controlled and pure, to be busy at home, to be kind, and to be subject to their husbands, so that no one will malign the word of God" (Titus 2:4–5 NIV). We need to be mentors and set the example of what a godly wife and mother should be. It is not necessary for us to have a degree in psychology or marriage and family. Younger women can learn much as we share our lifetime of experiences.

It is essential that the young women of today understand their God-given role in the family—that it is a great privilege to be a "helpmate" to our husbands.

We need to teach them to accept, approve, and affirm their husbands in the role that God has given them—the role of spiritual leadership of the family.

Nancy Binkley, mother of three, educational consultant, and Bible Study Fellowship teaching leader, gives this wise counsel: "In this new millennium more than in previous generations, young husbands and wives are working as teams to build strong families. In this spirit of cooperation and teamwork, it remains important for their children to continue to view dad as the provider and protector and respect him as such. They need to see that their mother is still viewed as the nurturer and heart of the home—that they cherish her role. With this balanced view, children are aided as they become the men and women God desires them to be."[8]

Submission: A Timeless Biblical Principle

Submission is a timeless biblical principal that is clearly laid out in Ephesians and Colossians (see Ephesians 5:22 and Colossians 3:18). It is an idea not thought up by men to keep wives in subjection, but rather comes from God himself. God's divine plan is for the husband to be the head and his wife the helpmate of the home (see Genesis 2:18). This is by no means a popular belief in our nation. It is an idea met with scorn and ridicule, especially from the feminists. Regardless of the "bad press" the practice of submission receives, biblical submission is God's order for the family.

The Women's Study Bible gives an excellent definition of what biblical submission means: "Submission means to put all of yourself—understandings, knowledge, opinions, feelings, energies—at the disposal of a person in authority over you. This never means subjecting yourself to abusive tyranny, nor does it suggest mindless acquiescence to the whims of another. . . . A wife's deference to her husband is a duty owed to the Lord. A wife's submission is not as much to her husband, a mere man, as it is to God and his plan for marriage."[9]

At the same time the women are being taught what God's Word says to them, the older men need to be teaching the younge men what God expects of the Christian husband—to "love your wives, just as Christ also loved the church and gave Himself for it" (Eph. 5:25 NKJV).

A home is to be filled with love—wife loving husband, husband loving wife, both loving their children. One expert has said, "A person who is loved at home does not need to seek proof elsewhere that they can be loved."[10] It was my deep desire that my children know how much I loved them and their father.

There are two questions every mother needs to ask on a regular basis: "Do my children know I'm crazy about them?" "Does my husband know I'm crazy about him?" If these questions cannot be answered in the affirmative, it is time to seek the Lord!

God *is* love. He wants us to truly love our families. He and he alone can enable us to love as he desires for us to love.

I wanted to love my children and my husband with the love of the Lord!

> We hand down our faith by principle . . . instructing
> our children in the ways of God.
> CHARLES STANLEY, *HOW TO KEEP YOUR KIDS ON YOUR TEAM*

Chapter 7

I Brought My Children Up "In the Nurture and Admonition of the Lord"

And, ye fathers, provoke not your children to wrath: but bring them up in the nurture and admonition of the Lord.

EPHESIANS 6:4 KJV

Having a godly heritage is one of my most valuable "possessions." I was privileged to grow up in a strong Christian home, to be brought up "in the nurture and admonition of the Lord." My heritage greatly influenced my child raising. I longed for my children to have a godly heritage too.

A United Pair

God gave me a wonderful Christian husband who had the same goals and desires I had for our children. We were in total agreement as to the way our children should be raised. Roland also had been brought up "in the nurture and admonition of the Lord." His life gave testimony to his godly training. He was a wonderful example to our children of how a Christian should live. His consistency was a shining light in our home. Our children could always look to their daddy for wisdom and instruction. They could safely follow his example in their dealings with others—at school, at church, and in the world. He is a man of integrity. His word is his bond. And his desire, like mine, was to bring up our children "in the nurture and admonition of the Lord."

"The Nurture and Admonition of the Lord"

This verse in Ephesians 6:4 was a Scripture my preacher granddaddy often quoted. What does this "old-fashioned sounding" Bible verse mean? What does it mean to bring children up in the "nurture and admonition of the Lord" (or in the "training and instruction of the Lord," as the New International Version states)? The word *nurture* is from the Greek word *paideia,* which means "to train up a child." As we nurture our children, we train them up in the ways of the Lord. The word *admonition* is from the Greek word *nouthesia,* which means "to call attention to; a mild rebuke or warning." The dictionary defines *admonition* in this way: "To counsel against wrong practices."[1] Therefore, if we seek to bring up our children in the "admonition of the Lord," our instruction will call attention to and counsel against those practices that the Bible declares are wrong. It will not be based on any so-called "expert" advice that contradicts God's Word. It will not be based on the thinking of man. Our instruction and training will be biblically based—

founded on God's Holy Word, the Bible. Second Timothy 3:16–17 gives us many compelling reasons for basing our lives on the Scriptures: "All Scripture is given by inspiration of God, and is profitable for doctrine, for reproof, for correction, for instruction in righteousness, that the man of God may be complete, thoroughly equipped for every good work" (NKJV). The New Living Translation states it as follows: "All Scripture is inspired by God and is useful to teach us what is true and to make us realize what is wrong in our lives. It straightens us out and teaches us to do what is right. It is God's way of preparing us in every way, fully equipped for every good thing God wants us to do."

Spiritual Development

Many parents are careful to see that their kids are enrolled in courses and activities that will enhance their mental and physical development. They run hither, thither, and yon so their children will "not miss out on anything." No development, however, is more fundamental to a Christian's life than spiritual development. In *Bringing Up Boys* Dr. James Dobson says:

Not only is spiritual development of relevance to eternity, it is also critical to the way your children will live out their days on this earth. Boys [and girls] need to be well established in their faith in order to understand the meaning of good and evil. They are growing up in a postmodern world in which all ideas are considered equally valid and nothing is really wrong. [To them] wickedness is bad only in the minds of those who think it is bad. People who live by this god-less outlook on life are headed for great pain and misery. The Christian worldview, by contrast, teaches that good and evil are determined by the God of the universe and that He has given us an unchanging moral standard by which to live. He also offers for-giveness from sins, which boys (and girls) have good reason to need. Only with this understanding is a child being prepared to face the challenges that lie ahead. Yet most American children receive no spiritual train-ing whatsoever![2]

Teaching our children the precepts of God's Holy Word is absolutely essential if our children are to develop a Christian worldview. It is crucial that they know the difference between right and wrong. If they are not brought up "in the training and instruc-tion of the Lord," they will be "headed for great pain and misery." They will not be prepared to face the imminent challenges of the postmodern world. Their spiritual development is of the utmost importance for now and for eternity.

Dr. Dobson's commentary on today's parents is staggering and sobering when he states: "Yet most American children receive no spiritual training what-soever."[3] George Barna, in a survey released in May 2003, stated: "Close to nine out of ten parents of children under age 13 (85%) believe they have the primary responsibility for the spiritual development of children, but few parents spend time during a typ-ical week interacting with their children on spiritual matters." According to the research, "parents typi-cally have no plan for the spiritual development of their children; do not consider it a priority, have little or no training in how to nurture a child's faith, have no related standards or goals they are seeking to satisfy, and experience no accountability for their efforts."[4]

Spiritual Development

The lack of spiritual development in children is obviously a monumental problem in today's world. It is one that must be addressed! Roland and I believed that the spiritual training and development of our children was the most significant "course" in which they would ever be enrolled. We also believed (and still do) that it is God's desire for *parents* to be the main teachers of this vital course. If our children are to have a biblically-based value system, we must assume the responsibility for their spiritual development. In his book *Children and Christian Faith,* Cos Davis says, "The family relationship, more than any other, is the basic influence on the value development of children."[5] Our "marching orders" are clear: We, as parents, must fulfill our God-given responsibility. We have a job to do!

Taking the First Step

What then is the first step? I believe Bible-based child-training begins with seeking to lead our children to a saving knowledge of Jesus Christ as Savior and Lord.

Every one of us is a sinner in need of the Savior, Jesus Christ. The Bible clearly spells this out for us in Romans 3:23: "For all have sinned and fall short of the glory of God" (NIV).

God loved us so much that he sent Jesus to die on the cross for our sins. Romans 5:8 states: "But God demonstrates his own love for us in this: While we were still sinners, Christ died for us" (NIV).

Through repentance of our sins and faith in Jesus Christ, we receive salvation—the gift of eternal life. In Romans 10:9 we read, "If you confess with your mouth, 'Jesus is Lord,' and believe in your heart that God raised him from the dead, you will be saved" (NIV).

"For God so loved the world, that he gave his only begotten Son, that whosoever believeth in him should not perish, but have everlasting life" (John 3:16 KJV).

John 1:12 states: "But as many as received him, to them gave he power to become to sons of God, even to them that believe on his name" (KJV).

Salvation is through Jesus Christ and him alone. Our children need to clearly understand this fact. In John 14:6 Jesus declared: "I am the way and the truth and the life. No one comes to the Father except through me" (NIV). In a day when many different paths are being presented as a way to God, how essential it is for our children to know that the Bible clearly teaches that Jesus is the *only* way to eternal life.

Parenthetically, because the most important decision a person makes is to trust Jesus Christ as Savior and Lord, we need to pray that our children will receive Jesus as Savior and Lord early in their lives. George Barna says: "Most of the people who accept Jesus Christ as their Savior do so at a young age."[6]

The Fear of the Lord

Bible-based child training—bringing our children up "in the nurture and admonition of the Lord"—also means helping them to develop a *reverential fear* of God, an awesome reverence for God. *The Women's Study Bible* describes the fear of God as "the attitude of reverent obedience."[7] Ecclesiastes 12:13 admonishes us: "Fear God and keep His commandments" (NKJV). Proverbs 14:27 says: "The fear of the LORD is a fountain of life, turning a man from the snares of death" (NIV).

John Witherspoon once said: "It is only the fear of God that can deliver us from the fear of man."[8]

I love what Patrick Morley, author of *I Surrender,* said about fearing the Lord. He couched it in everyday language so that even a child can understand its meaning. He stated: "The fear of the Lord is to love what God loves and to hate what God hates."[9] He went on to say that God loves wisdom and hates evil.[10] Proverbs 8:13 says: "To fear the LORD is to hate evil" (NIV). Psalm 111:10 tells us: "The fear of the LORD is the beginning of wisdom" (NKJV). If we truly *fear* the Lord, I believe we will have an "attitude of reverent obedience" toward God, and a desire to honor and obey our heavenly Father in all we do. We will love what he loves and hate what he hates. He is the sovereign Lord who reigns over all. He alone is worthy of our deep reverence and complete obedience.

Author Josh McDowell gives further emphasis to the importance of teaching our children to fear the Lord. He writes: "To develop a strong moral foundation within our young people we must teach them, first, to fear God, and secondly, to recognize him as the basis—the origin—of all truth."[11] Developing a strong moral foundation begins with developing a fear of the Lord. To learn what it means to fear the Lord is essential for both parents and children who desire to live godly, Christ-honoring, productive lives. He is the

Source—the only source—of all truth. Proverbs 1:7 tells us: "The fear of the LORD is the beginning of knowledge" (NIV).

Additional verses that extol the benefits of fearing the Lord are:

Psalm 85:9—"Surely his salvation is near those who fear him, that his glory may dwell in our land." (NIV)

Proverbs 16:6—"Through the fear of the LORD a man avoids evil." (NIV)

Proverbs 14:26–27 encourages us by stating: "He who fears the LORD has a secure fortress, and for his children it will be a refuge. The fear of the LORD is a fountain of life, turning a man from the snares of death." (NIV)

Proverbs 15:16 warns: "Better a little with the fear of the LORD than great wealth with turmoil." (NIV)

Psalm 25:12 assures us of God's guidance: "Who, then, is the man that fears the LORD? He will instruct him in the way chosen for him." (NIV)

Psalm 33:18–19 gives us great comfort: "But the eyes of the LORD are on those who fear him, on those whose hope is in his unfailing love, to deliver them from death and keep them alive in famine." (NIV)

Boundaries

What else must we do to train and instruct our children in the ways of God? I believe we must set high standards of conduct for our children—there must be definite boundaries. That was the practice

Roland and I followed in our home. The Holy Bible, with its moral absolutes, contained the set of standards on which we built our family boundaries and based all of our rules. Roland and I believed that not only do parents have a right to set boundaries, they have the responsibility to see that the boundaries are clearly defined and understood.

I agree with Gary Smalley and John Trent when they say: "Family boundaries are protective 'fences' put around a child for his security, support, and accountability. They give a child a sense of these things as he clearly sees limits on acceptable and unacceptable behavior. They also provide much-needed accountability when it comes to opening his life to positive people and experiences while closing the door to negative ones."[12] Family boundaries assist in teaching the child to say no to self and yes to God.

Boundaries help children to know they are loved. One way God communicates his love for us is by giving us protective boundaries and disciplining us if we go outside the fence of his Word. "The Lord disciplines those He loves," says Hebrews 12:6 (NIV). My husband and I set boundaries for our children—and tried to see that they were not breached because we loved our children too much *not* to do so.

It was encouraging to read in *Child* magazine that a professor at a liberal university in America was encouraging parents to set appropriate limits for their children in order to enhance the development of their children's character. Even the secular world acknowledges the importance of boundaries.

It would be foolish for me to leave the impression that our children *always* followed our rules, that they never crossed the boundaries. They, as is true of all

85

children, broke some of those rules. But they clearly *knew* the rules and understood they were to be followed. They understood the consequences of disobeying those rules. This was a vital part of our seeking to pass on our values to our kids.

Certain things were strictly off-limits at our house. For example, we had no alcohol or cigarettes in our home. R-rated movies and videos were not allowed. Certain kinds of music were taboo. Television was monitored very carefully. Because of my active involvement in fighting against the moral pollution inundating our nation, I was keenly aware of the dangers of too much TV and the detrimental effects certain television programs were having on our children.

The authors of *Tough-Minded Parenting* issue a straightforward warning to parents and grandparents under the heading: "Prime Time TV—a Clear and Present Danger": "Television is the anti-vision medium. Children are constantly being removed from their home values as effectively as though they were taken for several months of every year to another world. Few parents would knowingly choose this world of negative values. We are often so careful about the day care, the preschool, the friends, and other examples our children will see. Why, then, do we turn them over to the passive television baby-sitter who fills their minds with uselessness and harmful examples of how to live?"[13]

Josh McDowell's assessment should be a wake-up call for us all. He says, "Movies and TV present a totally unrealistic model of actions and consequences. But more poisonous still is the impact of a daily diet of characters and shows that display little distinction between right and wrong and little relationship between a person's actions and the consequences that result from his or her behavior."[14]

At our house, television programs were carefully screened. And one more thing: the same movies, videos, and television programs that were off-limits to our kids were also off-limits to us, their parents. If our kids shouldn't view something, neither should we. There was not one set of standards for the kids and another for the adults!

Maddoxes' Laws

As long as our children lived under our roof, daddy's rules were to be followed. These were affectionately called "Maddoxes' Laws." Roland has always said that he believes in the "golden rule"—"He who has the gold makes the rules." He also believes in the Golden Rule from God's Word—"In everything, do to others what you would have them do to you" (Matt. 7:12 NIV).

One of my husband's rules was that every boy our daughter dated had to be interviewed first by her daddy. To many of today's teenagers, that might sound unbelievable and unreasonable, but it served as a protection for our daughter and turned out to be a positive aspect of her life. Those young men respected her dad and, in turn, respected his daughter. I recall one young man who walked the length of a high school gym to shake hands with my husband, even though the boy and our daughter were no longer dating. He and my husband had established a relationship of friendship and respect.

Moral Absolutes

Today, many parents fail to see the need for setting boundaries for their children or teaching them the difference between right and wrong. They have no moral absolutes. How tragic! In this day of permissiveness, my husband's and my way of life during our children's maturing years may seem strict to some observers. But the facts of sin and its devastating consequences were always prevalent in our minds. We knew that our children might not always *do* what was right, but they would always *know* what was right.

Teaching children the difference between right and wrong is absolutely essential for Christian parents. The Bible is still our authority—the moral absolutes in the Bible are true in the day in which we live. The Ten Commandments have not become merely "suggestions for living." We may not be able to display them in the public square, but they must still be written on our hearts and practiced in our lives. God gave them to Moses for a reason. God knew what man needed. His commands were given out of his great love for us. They were given for our good.

In their outstanding book *The Ways of God,* Henry Blackaby and Roy Edgemon tell us: "The Father's commands bring life. They are not legalistic demands from an angry God. A command from the Father is an invitation from perfect love to see more of God's love than you have ever known. . . . God's commands, like every word from God, are a gift to you from the One who loves you most."[15]

Obedience Brings Blessing

God's commands were his gift to us, his children, given because of his great love for us. My husband and I set high standards for our kids because of our great love for them. We wanted God's best for them. We wanted them to avoid all the heartache possible.

We knew obedience to the Lord's commands brings blessings. Disobedience results in negative consequences and sorrow. As we instilled within them God's truths—biblical precepts—we prayed that, as a result, they would be kept from sin and suffering. We wanted them to have a thirst for God's Word and the discipline to study it. Our great desire was for them to walk in God's truth all the days of their lives.

The "Hidden" Word

We prayed that not only would they come to love God's Word, they also would learn it. To reinforce our teachings and our beliefs, we knew they must hide God's Word in their hearts. Once they left home, we would no longer be there to instruct and teach. They needed to have the Scriptures "at their fingertips," to give them wisdom and help in the many challenging circumstances they would face. Psalm 119:11 says: "Your word I have hidden in my heart, that I might not sin against You" (NKJV).

In an online survey entitled "Parents Accept Responsibility for Their Child's Spiritual Development but Struggle with Effectiveness," George Barna states: "Although parents are generally unaware of how their children are doing in terms of spiritual development, the survey indicated that the two areas that parents acknowledged as weaknesses for their children were: knowing how to study the Bible and memorizing Bible verses."[16] I believe one of the most significant things we did for our children was to see that they memorized Scriptures, beginning at an early age. Those verses our children learned when they were young have stayed with them all their lives. Psalm 119:105 assures us:

"Your word is a lamp to my feet and a light to my path" (NKJV).

I shall never forget what a dear friend—who had come to know the Lord Jesus as an adult—said to me: "I am so jealous of your storehouse of memorized Scriptures. I would give anything if I had learned all those verses as a child. I spend so much time trying to find where a verse is located in my Bible." What a great gift to give your child—the gift of seeing to it that he memorizes Scripture. It will be a gift that never stops giving.

The Model of Deuteronomy Six

What are some other things we can institute in our homes as we seek to instill God's principles in our children's lives, bringing them up "in the training and instruction of the Lord"? I believe we are to follow the model of Deuteronomy 6: Moses said: "These commandments that I give you today are to be upon your hearts. Impress them on your children. Talk about them when you sit at home and when you walk along the road, when you lie down and when you get up. Tie them as symbols on your hands and bind them on your foreheads. Write them on the doorframes of your houses and on your gates" (Deut. 6:6–9 NIV).

In commenting on the practical outworking of this verse, Ruth Ann VanderSteeg, mother of five adult children, all of whom are serving the Lord, wrote:

> We included the Lord Jesus in our conversations; we prayed all the time about everything—from lost car keys to a car that wouldn't start in the middle of an intersection, to praise and thanksgiving for life, for family, for a beautiful day. In praying for big

things and small things, we talked to God
and they learned to hear from him. We
included the Lord Jesus in our conversations,
not just at 'appropriate times,' but in our
everyday conversations. We taught them
that Jesus was their Savior, their Lord, and
their very best friend, because that is what
he is to us. We never kept that quiet; we
talked about him continually.[17]

Importance of the Family Altar

One effective instrument we used to carry out the
commands of Deuteronomy 6 was the family altar—a
time of family worship. We explored many different
options for this time together. Of course it changed
with the differing ages and stages. We used a series of
books entitled *Little Visits with God* when our children
were small. They loved these books. As they grew older,
we did a lot of teaching from the book of Proverbs.
When the children were preteens, one day a week they
would be in charge of this time of family worship. We
have some special memories of those days. Although it
was hard to find time to worship as a family when all
the activities for the children were in full swing, we
kept on trying to observe this time. As I look back, it
was definitely worth the effort.

Building Character Into Your Children

It is always a "good time" to build character in
your children. Use every opportunity as a teaching and
learning opportunity. Using Proverbs to teach basic
character traits is an excellent place to begin (and stay
for long periods of time). There are also many good
books available on character building today. Since so

few books were available in the seventies, I devised lessons of my own. The impartation of our values was of the utmost importance to us as parents.

Prayer—An Essential Ingredient

Prayer was an integral part of our family worship time. We had a large, circular coffee table that was only twelve inches above the floor. At night our family gathered around it to pray. It was used on many other occasions for the same purpose. Many prayers ascended to the Father from that spot in our den. Time and again we saw God's answers to the prayers that were offered there. When our son moved into his own home, this table meant so much to him that he asked if he could take it with him. We were thrilled with his request. It had truly become a special place of family prayer.

Our dear friends the Orman Simmonses began a special Sunday night family prayer time when their three daughters reached middle school and high school age. After church, Mom and Dad would gather with the girls and talk about the week ahead. Then they would list prayer requests from each member of the family. All during the week they could pray for each other. The following Sunday evening, they met again to see how God had answered and blessed that week. Then they prayed for the upcoming week. What a great idea!

It is easy for parents to rush the nighttime prayer and worship time with the kids because of time constraints and weariness. However, to do so on a regular basis will convey to the children that this nightly event is not very important for you or for them. This, of course, is the opposite of what you want to teach.

Work hard to rearrange schedules to protect this precious family time. You will never regret it. When your children are gone, you will long for these special times with them.

Goal of Bible-Based Child Training

The goal of Bible-based child training is to develop mature Christian adults whose lives are grounded in God's Word—young adults with a biblical worldview whose lives reflect their beliefs. In March 1993, in Dallas, Texas, forty-two Christian youth leaders met with Josh McDowell in a symposium examining the state of the youth culture. For more than two days they sought to determine the most pressing problems of today's youth and the best ways of addressing this generation. "One hundred percent of the participants ranked this generation's loss of a biblically-based value system as their number one concern."[18]

In his latest book, *Bringing Up Boys,* Dr. James Dobson recalls that when he was writing a previous book for young people entitled *Life on the Edge,* his publisher assembled focus groups in different cities to "determine the stress points and needs of the younger generation."[19] He further shares the sad observation from this study: "Most of the young people with whom we talked found it difficult to answer questions such as 'Who am I as a person?' 'How did I get here?' 'Is there a right or wrong way to believe and act?' 'How do I achieve eternal life, if it exists?' 'What is the meaning of life and death?' . . . They had only a vague notion of what we might call 'first truths.' No wonder they lacked a sense of meaning and purpose. Life loses its significance for a person who has no understanding of his origin or destination."[20]

He goes on to comment:

Human beings tend to struggle with troubling questions they can't answer. Just as nature abhors a vacuum, so the intellect acts to fill the void. Or to state it differently, it seeks to repair a hole in its system of beliefs. That is why so many young people today chase after twisted and alien "theologies," such as New Age nonsense, the pursuit of pleasure, substance abuse and illicit sex. They are searching vainly for something that will satisfy their "soul hunger." They are unlikely to find it. Not even great achievement and superior education will put the pieces together. Meaning in life comes only by answering the eternal questions listed above, and they are adequately addressed only in the Christian faith. No other religion can tell us who we are, how we got here, and where we are going after death. And no other belief system teaches that we are known and loved individually by the God of the universe and by His only Son, Jesus Christ. . . .

That brings us back to the subject of boys and what they and their sisters need from parents during the developmental years. At the top of the list is an understanding of who God is and what He expects them to do. This teaching must begin very early in childhood.[21]

As I read those significant words, I thought about my own children. My husband and I certainly did not do everything right in our child raising, but I was thankful that we began early in their childhood to seek to bring them up in the "nurture and admonition of the Lord." We did everything we could to help them develop a strong belief system based on the Bible—an understanding of who God is and what he expected of them. We sought to help them embrace strong Christian values and develop convictions built upon God and his Word. He was their sure foundation. His Word would be their compass.

The Trustworthiness of Our God

Foundational to our children's lives was their understanding of the trustworthiness and faithfulness of their God. He is utterly trustworthy. He is absolutely faithful. He is omnipotent, omnipresent, and omniscient. Thus we taught them to "trust in the LORD with all your heart and lean not on your own understanding; in all your ways acknowledge him, and he will make your paths straight" (Prov. 3:5–6 NIV). But would our children learn to follow the admonition of the writer of Proverbs if we as parents were not following it ourselves? The answer is *no*. It is one thing to preach to our children that they should fear the Lord, trust the Lord, and obey him. It is quite another to practice what we preach.

Practicing what we preached was a constant challenge to us.

Roland and I sought to bring up our children "in the nurture and admonition of the Lord— in the training and instruction of our God."

No matter where they [my children] might be, they knew I *could* pray for them. No matter the circumstances, they knew I *would* pray for them.

SARAH MADDOX, *A MOTHER'S GARDEN OF PRAYER*

Chapter 8

I Constantly Prayed for My Children

"Arise, cry out in the night, as the watches of the night begin; pour out your heart like water in the presence of the LORD. Lift up your hands to him for the lives of your children."

LAMENTATIONS 2:19 NIV

God's School of Prayer

For more than forty years I have been enrolled in "God's School of Prayer." I have repeated a "course" entitled "Praying for Your Children" year after year. Although the course title has remained the same, the lessons often have been new and difficult. My Master Teacher has been so patient with me—prodding me, admonishing me, scolding me, forgiving me when my prayers were selfish or self-serving. It has been an incredible education—a lifelong learning process.

Prayer Requests

The prayer requests have changed as the stages of our children's lives have changed. When our children were babies, it was their health and behavior that concerned me. With Melanie being sick so often, I found myself constantly praying that she would get well and stay well. With Alan's arrival two and a half years after Melanie was born, I needed to pray for the two young siblings as they learned to relate to each other. As the "terrible twos" came upon us, I found that my prayers were often for myself—that I might have the wisdom, patience, and strength necessary to deal with two preschoolers. As school days arrived, my prayer partners and I prayed for our children's protection—physical, mental, emotional, and spiritual. We prayed for their relationships with their peers and for their teachers and coaches. We earnestly prayed that each child, at an early age, would come to know Jesus Christ personally as Savior and Lord.

As their days in middle school dawned, we added to our prayer list prayers concerning the changes that were taking places in their bodies and in their relationships. We prayed for physical and spiritual growth. We prayed that each would be protected from being victimized, abducted, or molested. We prayed that both would have a heart for God.

(*Note:* When your children are old enough to understand, it is important that they know you are praying for them. Ask them to give you their requests and share with them the answers! This is one way you are teaching them the value of prayer in your life and in theirs. If they come in and interrupt your time of prayer once in a while, you can use that "disruptive moment" as an opportunity to pray with them, to talk with them about your prayer time and theirs, and to hear their prayer requests.)

During my children's teenage years, I found myself often on my knees. Sometimes my knees were not low enough. I had to fall on my face, crying out to the Lord on behalf of my children. I knew it was my responsibility to stand in the gap for them. There are so many emotional upheavals in the teenage years, both for the teenager and his parents. Only a praying mother can find the stability and wisdom to handle each situation. Even a praying mother sometimes finds herself "at the end of her rope." It is then that we are comforted by a wonderful verse in Romans. It tells us that when we don't know how to pray, the Holy Spirit will intercede for us: "In the same way, the Spirit helps us in our weakness. We do not know what we ought to pray for, but the Spirit himself intercedes for us with groans that words cannot express" (Rom. 8:26 NIV).

All too soon our first child went off to college, to a school far from home. I knew, however, that my prayers would reach across the miles from Tennessee to Texas. Seven of us mothers formed a special prayer group to pray for our college kids. It was such a blessing. When one of us did not know how to pray, the others always seemed to come up with the appropriate petitions. We came to love one another's children dearly as we interceded for them frequently and earnestly. We laughed together and cried together. We claimed promises and stood firmly on God's Word. Many times we found ourselves in "God's Waiting Room." The words of Isaiah 64:4 were a constant encouragement to our hearts: "For since the beginning of the world men have not heard nor perceived by the ear, nor has the eye seen any God besides You, Who acts for the one who waits for Him" (NKJV).

Keep on Asking, Keep on Seeking, Keep on Knocking

I once thought that the teenage years were the hardest for mothers. (That was when I was going through them with my kids.) But in my case, and in the case of many moms I know, it was the years just following the teenage years that were the most difficult. Why? Because it was such an unsettled time for our kids, and thus often unsettling for us as their mothers. I also discovered that as my children grew into adulthood, when things in their lives got "broken," I could not "fix" them. They were adults. They had to be responsible for fixing those things in their lives that were falling apart. I was there to counsel and advise when needed. I was always there to support and love them. And I could be called on to pray for them at any time of the day or night. But I was no longer responsible for solving their problems and "picking up the pieces" in their lives.

Aaron and Hur

The Bible encourages us to go into our prayer closets alone, but it also admonishes us to join with others in prayer. Two verses stand out in particular:

Matthew 18:20: "Where two or three are gathered together in my name, there am I in the midst of them." (KJV)

Psalm 55:18–19: "He will redeem my soul in peace from the battle which is against me, for there are many who strive with me. God will hear and answer them." (NASB)

It was my mother who first encouraged me to pray regularly for my children with other Christian mothers—to gather together in the name of Jesus. I owe her a great debt of gratitude. She taught me that everyone needs "an Aaron and a Hur" to hold up her arms in prayer. This idea, of course, comes from the story in Exodus 17. Moses, Aaron, and Hur had gone up on the Mount of God so Moses could intercede for Joshua during his battle with the Amalekites. As Moses prayed for Joshua, he held up the rod of God. As long as he was able to hold up the rod, Joshua was victorious over Amalek and his forces. When Moses's hands got tired, he lowered the rod and Joshua began to lose the battle. Aaron and Hur came to the rescue! Aaron held up one of Moses's arms and Hur held up the other, and the battle was won!

I, too, needed "an Aaron and a Hur." My children were facing a daily spiritual battle—a battle for their minds and hearts. Intercessory prayer for my children was a necessity. They needed me to intercede for them every day of their lives—sometimes every hour of the day. Prayer partners were a wonderful support in this daily battle against Satan and the world. We could not always be with our kids in their daily encounters, but we could always hold them up to the Father in prayer. And we did. Long ago I came to believe that the public battles in which our children were engaged would more likely be won if we as mothers were on our knees, privately interceding for them on a regular basis. In Ezekiel 22:30 we read: "I looked for a man among them who would build up the wall and stand before me in the gap on behalf of the land so I would not have to destroy it, but I found none" (NIV). Our children need desperately for us to stand in the gap for them.

Intercessory Prayer

God is looking for intercessors—for mothers who will stand in the gap on behalf of their families. We might say that intercession is love in prayer. It is love bowing the knee on behalf of those whom we love. It is not an easy task. It requires effort, determination, and perseverance. We must seek to pray in accordance with God's will for each child. Our prayers are to be God-authored, not momma-authored.

As we come to our heavenly Father, seeking what we should pray for our loved ones, he will reveal to us his plans and purposes. "Prayer takes us into God's presence . . . shows us His will."[1]

To me, one of the saddest verses in all of the Bible is found in Isaiah 59:16: "And He [the Lord] . . . was astonished that there was no one to intercede" (NASB). I wonder how many times God has been astonished that we are not interceding for our children? We wring our hands and worry ourselves sick about our children's difficult circumstances. We talk to our friends and family, and then, often as a last resort, go to the Lord. I was really convicted when I read Paul Powell's book *A Faith that Sings*. He says, "The rankest form of humanism is prayerlessness. When a person chooses not to pray, he is choosing to go it on his own by his own human resources. He is saying, 'I can get along without God in my life.'"[2]

When we do *not* pray, are we not in effect saying, "God, I can handle this by myself. I don't need your help." Samuel once cried: "As for me, far be it from me that I should sin against the LORD by ceasing to pray for you" (1 Sam. 12:23 NASB).

The Power of Prayer

While these indictments *convict* us, the inexpressible power available to us when we do pray should *convince* us to turn from prayerlessness to a life of intercession. As Christians, through the resurrected Lord Jesus Christ, we have immediate accessibility to the most amazing resource—the mighty resource available to every believer—the *dunamis* (dynamite) power of God! As we pray for our children, God's miraculous power is released in their lives! Our prayers bring God into our situations!

Sidlow Baxter, in *Awake My Heart,* sets forth the unbelievable "potential" of our secret daily prayer audience with God when he says: "That secret daily session alone with God is greater than all merely human deliberations because it brings God into things. . . . It may seem difficult to think that one humble Christian believer, kneeling in a small room in secret prayer, can wield an influence outmatching that of ostentatious state counsels [but] the decisions of deliberate bodies and the whole course of events can be affected by such praying."[3]

I am convinced that we ought to be going to God, standing in the gap for our children—praying for them morning, noon, and night. The psalmist said in Psalm 55:17: "Evening, and morning, and at noon, will I pray, and cry aloud: and he shall hear my voice" (KJV). God invites us to come boldly to the throne of grace to summon his power for our personal problems. We are not to come timidly. We are not to come faintheartedly. We are to come boldly, expectantly, seeking his mercy and his help in time of need—asking that his power be released in every situation.

Ephesians 3:20 states, "Now unto him that is able to do exceedingly abundantly above all that we ask or think, according to the power that worketh in us . . ." (KJV). Remember: God's power is always available to us! The question we must ask is, "Are we always available to be the conduits of his power?"

The Impact of Prayer

A part of passing on our beliefs and values to our children should include teaching *them* the value of prayer. We should make abundantly clear the importance we place on praying for them. Sharing with them answered prayer, especially when it affects them, is so important. Not only should our children know that we are praying for them, but from the time our children can talk, we ought to be teaching *them* to pray. Often, we may feel they are too young to fully understand what is happening, but it may surprise us at what they actually comprehend.

I recently heard the story of a kindergarten-aged church group called Mission Friends going on a "prayer walk" in downtown Nashville, Tennessee. Some observers wondered if they weren't too young to understand what they were doing. Several days later one of those five-year-olds was in the car with her mother in the same area of town where the group had gone on their "prayer walk." Suddenly the youngster looked up at one of the buildings and said: "Mother, we better stop and pray—there are some people in that building who don't know Jesus." Obviously that child was not too young to be taught about the importance of prayer and to be involved in praying for others. Your child can learn about prayer even before he learns to talk. Model it before him. He will quickly follow your example.

For years I have been speaking on the subject "Praying for Your Children." I was asked several times to speak on this subject at my home church. But it was not until just a few years ago that I heard my daughter speak about the difference it had made in her life to have had her mother praying for her.

In her own words while speaking to Bellevue Baptist Church's women's ministry, our daughter, Melanie Redd, said:

> What difference did it make that my mother prayed for me? For me, it made a lot of difference. I believe in prayer. I believe prayer works. I think I've seen it, felt it, tasted it, heard it, experienced it, smelled it. I'm convinced that just talking to God does make a difference. It is a simple act; it doesn't seem sometimes like you are doing very much when you pray; it really doesn't always feel like much is going on. And yet you are doing battle for what's ahead. And I believe in the power of prayer because someone prayed for me. I watched the answers to prayer, and my kids are learning that now. That is something I'm going to pass along. I also think that I pray more personally because I was prayed for and was taught to pray. I believe in prayer, and so I pray.

The Joyful Results of Prayer

On the way to my precious mother's funeral in 1999, I was looking in her personal Bible for Scriptures that could be read at her funeral. Many, many verses were underlined, but my attention was drawn to the following verses in Psalm 105 which seemed to characterize my mother's life.

Glory in his holy name;
let the hearts of those who seek the LORD
rejoice.
Look to the LORD and his strength;
seek his face always. (vv. 3–4 NIV)

My mother was a rejoicing woman all of her days. Why was she such a joyful woman? I believe it was because she had looked to the Lord for his strength in every situation; she had gloried in his holy name; she had sought his face always—she was a woman of prayer. And because she was a woman of prayer, she taught me the value of a consistent prayer life—the joy of spending much time in the presence of the Lord.

You and I will find joy unspeakable as we spend daily time in his presence, interceding for our precious children. The psalmist gives voice to this truth as he speaks to our heavenly Father in Psalm 16:11: "You have made known to me the path of life; you will fill me with joy in your presence, with eternal pleasures at your right hand" (NIV).

I have experienced this joy as I have prayed constantly for my children all of their lives— and continue to do so daily.

The best inheritance a father can leave his
children is a good example.
GOD'S LITTLE INSTRUCTION BOOK

Chapter 9

My Husband and I Took Our Children to Sunday School and Church

<table>
<tr><td>

~

"And let us consider
one another . . .not
forsaking the assem-
bling of ourselves
together."

HEBREWS 10:24–25 NKJV

~
</td><td>

*Setting the
Right Example*
</td></tr>
</table>

It seems there have always
been young adults who, at
some time earlier in their lives,
decided that Sunday school
was just for children. Therefore, when they became
parents, they did not see the need to be a part of a Bible
class on Sunday mornings. Many of these parents,
especially the dads, would drop off their kids at a
church or send them with someone else. Some of them
would join their children for the church service; others
didn't attend at all. What a colossal mistake this was!

These parents were building into their children's minds the idea that Bible study was just for kids. Their kids would probably come to the conclusion that they didn't need to incorporate Bible study into their adult lifestyles either.

Although many churches no longer have Bible study groups on Sunday morning, I encourage everyone to find a way to study the Bible in a group every week. It might take the form of a cell group or a Bible study at church, school, or the office. This will be a valuable part of the week, even if one's church does not provide for adult Bible study on Sunday mornings.

Ignorance and Indifference

Today, many young adults have turned their backs not only on Sunday school/Bible study but also on regular church attendance. A minister once shared with me that in the fifties and sixties, many Christian parents centered their lives around their churches— around the work of Jesus Christ. But today it seems that church attendance is just one more thing on their long list of things they do. If it fits into their busy schedules, they will attend. If it doesn't fit, they won't come. Their lives are centered around themselves and their families—not around their churches or the Lord Jesus Christ. As a result, we are witnessing a generation *ignorant* of biblical information and *indifferent* to spiritual things.

We as parents have a tremendous responsibility to educate our children in spiritual matters. Some evangelical seminaries call this "spiritual formation." I believe that the spiritual formation of our children should begin in the very earliest years of their lives. For this to happen, we must set the example for our children. We cannot expect them to be interested in the things of God if we have communicated the opposite messages with our lifestyles.

Church Attendence: A Requirement at Our House

My husband and I *took* our children to church; church attendance was a requirement at our house. We required them to brush their teeth, go to bed on time, be honest—all of these things were for their good. Why should we not require them to go to church? It was certainly an exercise for their good! But we went a step further. We tried never to make them feel it was a duty to attend church, but rather a privilege. We loved our church—we loved our pastor and the people there. We centered our lives around our church and its ministries. We taught our children to do the same. Today both of them are actively involved in their churches—not because they have to be but because they want to be.

Home and Church Working Together

In his book *Children and the Christian Faith* Cos Davis points out: "The home and the church should work together to teach religious values to children. They are partners, not competitors in this venture. The home is the informal center for teaching values. The church is the center of formal instruction."[1]

I believe every Christian family ought to seek a church they can love, one in which they can invest their time, money, and talents in the service of their Lord. It should be a church that preaches the Word of God and magnifies Jesus Christ in all of its programs.

We should want our children to hear the truth from the pulpit and in the Sunday school classes, to be in a loving environment where Jesus Christ is praised and exalted. There are wonderful Bible-believing evangelical Christian churches throughout the world. It is essential to find such a church.

Fellowship

Why do I think that church attendance is so important for a family? First of all, because God commands us not to forsake "the assembling of ourselves together" (Heb. 10:25 KJV). This verse in the New International Version is translated in more modern terms: "Let us not give up meeting together." We need to meet with other Christians in fellowship and worship on a regular basis. We need the support of our Christian friends. They need our support. What a blessing it is to spend time with other believers in worship, study, prayer, and praise. The psalmist declared in Psalm 5:7: "But I, by your great mercy, will come into your house; in reverence will I bow down toward your holy temple" (NIV).

Getting Fed Spiritually

Another reason—and a major one—for attending a Bible-believing church is for the spiritual food received there. It is important to hear from God on the first day of the week. There are so many other messages bombarding our senses all week long; the world gets its messages across day and night. Above the clamor of the world, God wants us to hear and understand his message to us. Henry Blackaby, in the workbook *Experiencing God,* says: "You cannot know the truth of your situation until you have heard from

God."[2] We need to use every opportunity possible to focus on his Word—to hear a Word from God. The only way we can keep the world from "squeezing us into its own mold"[3] is by consistent worship, study of God's Word, and quality time in prayer. When we spend time with him, God will give us the courage and strength to face the many onslaughts the world heaves at us day after day. Spiritual nourishment is essential for a Christian to stay spiritually strong. A wonderful verse in Colossians gives us a formula for a strong Christian faith: "And now, just as you accepted Christ Jesus as your Lord, you must continue to live in obedience to him. Let your roots grow down into him and draw up nourishment from him, so you will grow in faith, strong and vigorous in the truth you were taught" (Col. 2:6–7 NLT). A good church helps to provide this nourishment. Rick Warren, speaking of the church family in *The Purpose-Driven Life* says, "We grow faster and stronger by learning from each other and being accountable to each other."[4]

Role Models

There are some other reasons I advocate regular church attendance. Through the years I have seen that one of the most effective instruments God uses to accomplish his purposes in our lives is the Bible-believing, Bible-preaching, Christ-honoring local church. For example, what a tremendous positive influence Sunday school teachers can have on your child's life. In a day when so many negative forces seek to engulf our children, drawing them away from God, a godly Sunday school teacher can have quite an impact. When we look back at our own childhood days, my husband

Roland and I both can recall women teachers who told captivating Bible stories that whetted our appetites for spiritual things. Roland often speaks of the godly influence of the male Sunday school teachers under whose teaching he sat as a teenager. They were men of strong Christian convictions who loved kids and were excellent role models in their businesses as well as with their families. They truly impacted his life. The direction of my life was greatly influenced by some gracious and godly women Sunday school teachers under whose teaching I was privileged to sit as a teenager and young adult.

In our own children's lives, I praise God for the many godly young men and women in our church who were such positive examples to them. These young people were the kinds of role models we so longed for our children to have. Melanie speaks of the many women whom God sent to counsel and mentor her. One young woman in particular encouraged my seventh grade daughter to remain pure until marriage. She studied the Bible with Melanie for many months. Melanie followed her example. Today our daughter is a popular speaker for junior high and high school girls on the very subject of purity.

Our son had two youth workers in our church who helped to steer the course of his life. One was a junior high youth minister who spent time with our son as a seventh grader. I can still see them working in our driveway on the minister's old car. Alan was a superb mechanic. It was what he enjoyed doing. While they were working on his car, Rusty was sharing strong Christian principles and ideas that reinforced what we were teaching at home.

Later on, the singles' minister in our church had a greater impact on our son's life than anyone else other than Alan's dad. (Alan has always said his dad was his number one hero!) This minister truly understood young adults and knew how to relate to them. He talked straight with them, and they listened. Today that minister is one of the outstanding pastors in our denomination. Our son still looks up to him and is grateful that God put him in his life just when he needed him. Had we not been active in this particular church, they probably would never have even known each other.

Regular Church Attendence Sets the Stage for Future Generations

Ruth Ann VanderSteeg states: "The greatest benefit I can tell that my children received from regular church attendance and participation is to see them raising their children, my grandchildren, in like manner.

- It has given their families consistency and stability.
- It teaches the family discipline.
- It teaches the family to worship the Lord together with other believers.
- It teaches them gratefulness for a godly pastor who continually teaches the truth of the Word of God.
- It gives them confidence in knowing the Word of God so that they can share with others—not out of pride but out of gratefulness for what God has done for them and how much he loves mankind.

- It has helped them to realize their own spiritual gifts and has given them opportunity to use them.
- It has also been a great benefit to see them find their friends among the body of believers and in some cases their spouses.
- It has taught them the benefits of walking with the wise."[5]

George Barna always has interesting relevant statistics. He once asked teens to evaluate the church-based ministry they received as children. Here are the results:

A majority of teenagers—56%—said that they attended church-related activities an average of two or more times per month prior to turning 13. When asked what they learned from their exposure to the church's ministry while they were young children and adolescents, 8 out of 10 identified something that they felt was an important insight or category of lessons.

Three of the outcomes were claimed by nine out of ten teens:

- having had exposure to Bible stories (95%)
- learning about the lives of great people in the Bible (92%)
- having fun or positive experiences related to religion (89%)

Nearly as many young people said they felt they had

- developed meaningful friendships at church, (85%),
- developed a deeper relationship with Jesus Christ (85%),

- had opportunities to serve needy people alongside of their churched peers (85%).[6]

Help Wanted

Parents need all the help they can get in raising godly offspring. When my husband and I were growing up, our parents received reinforcement at school and at church. In the public schools Roland and I attended, Christian principles were upheld and honored. Today many fine Christian teachers are in the public school system, but they cannot read the Bible or overtly teach Christian principles to their classes. The church emerges as an even more important force in the lives of our families, serving as a reinforcement of what we are trying to impart at home.

The Electives

There is one more thing I would like to add about the importance of family church attendance and participation. I am so grateful for the outstanding programs our church provided for our kids' physical, mental, and emotional growth and development. There were sports programs; teams of all kinds were sponsored by our church. There were fantastic music programs—choirs and choir trips, orchestra, handbells, etc. All of these activities helped to work against the everflowing pipeline of evil and negativism our kids were hearing day after day. So much of secular music sends unbelievably bad messages to our kids. Good Christian music helps to counteract this godless influence.

The Bible memory program our church started was in response to our request as parents to equip our children over and above what we could have done on our own. Men's and women's ministries provided support groups and valuable seminars on marriage and family for us parents. Vacation Bible schools have long been a fantastic training ground—an integral part of the summer's activities for the children.

Surely you can see why we thought it was important to take our children to Sunday school (or Bible study) on Sundays and to participate in the activities of our church all during the week. Listen to what George Barna discovered in his survey about taking children to church: "Adults who attended church as a child are twice as likely as others to read the Bible during a typical week; twice as likely to attend a church worship service in a typical week; and nearly 50% more likely to pray to God during a typical week."[7]

The Accountability Factor

This is another survey of Barna's however, that is disturbing. The Mississippi Baptist Record reported: "The words of George Barna ought to be a wake-up call for parents in the twenty-first century. In speaking to a group of ministers in Mississippi in the fall of 2003, Barna reported that his research shows: 'Only 9 percent of born-again adults have a biblical world view. Another 6 percent have the foundation—a belief that there is absolute moral truth and that the Bible is the source of truth. That means 85 percent of all born again adults have neither the foundation nor the theological perspective required for a biblical world view,' he pointed out."[8] What a sad commentary! This should make us parents sit up and ask some probing questions: Is my church's program for young people having the impact it needs to have? Are my kids really learning and internalizing biblical truths? Am I, as a parent, supporting the youth leaders of my church?

Josh McDowell also addresses this problem in his book entitled *Beyond Belief to Convictions*. The subtitle reads: *What You Need to Know to Help Youth Stand Strong in the Face of Today's Culture.* He says:

> While we need to fear what our kids could be tempted to do, we need to be more concerned with what our kids are led to believe. You see, the way our kids behave comes from something. Their attitudes and actions spring from their value system, and their value system is based on what they believe. . . . Our kids, even those from solid Christian homes and churches, have distorted beliefs about God and the Bible, beliefs that are having a devastating rippling effect into every aspect of their lives.[9]

It takes both a Christ-centered home and a Christ-honoring church to instill within a child a strong biblical worldview. Christian education must begin at home at a very early age, and the church must reinforce the beliefs that are taught at home. As important as the praise and worship services are, if our churches are to have a lasting impact on our kids, they must provide weekly opportunities for deep and life-changing Bible study. If kids do not know what God's Word teaches, if they do not know what they believe and why, how can they counteract the onslaught of false teaching that constantly bombards them?

Parents and churches have the responsibility of seeing that their youth do not grow up with "distorted beliefs about God and the Bible." Both need to seek to develop within each child a strong biblical worldview. I am truly grateful for the evangelical Christian churches in our nation that are standing firmly against the tide of secular humanism and postmodernism. All of us must be accountable to one another.

We did not "forsake the assembling of ourselves" with other Christians on a regular basis. It was a habit formed years ago, which our children are continuing in their own families.

> Surrender is best demonstrated in
> obedience and trust.
> RICK WARREN, *THE PURPOSE-DRIVEN LIFE*

Chapter 10

I Was Willing to Let Go and Let God Have His Way in Their Lives

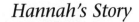

"But I trust in you, O LORD; I say, 'You are my God.' My times are in your hands."

PSALM 31:14–15 NIV

Hannah's Story

The story of Hannah is a wonderful Old Testament narrative that has been a marvelous example to mothers and "want-to-be" mothers through the years. We first see Hannah's unabated longing for a child. Then comes her earnest petition to the Lord, with the accompanying promise to give the child back to the Lord for all the days of his life. God answers her fervent prayers. A child is born to her and her husband, Elkanah. They name the child Samuel. As Hannah promised, when Samuel is weaned, she brings him to the house of the Lord at Shiloh to return him to the One who had given her the precious "gift." As she presents Samuel to Eli the priest, she says, as recorded in 1 Samuel 1:27–28: "I prayed for this child, and the LORD has granted me what I asked of him. So now I give him to the LORD. For his whole life he will be given over to the LORD" (NIV). Hannah serves as an example to all mothers because she truly "let go and let God" have his way in Samuel's life.

Letting Go and Letting God

Letting go and letting God have his way is often difficult because it involves surrender—the surrender of someone or some thing. For Hannah, it meant the surrender of her only child. Surrender is often painful—especially when it encompasses sacrifice. This was indeed a sacrifice for Hannah; she was giving up what she had wanted more than anything else— a son. She would not get to raise him in their home. He would grow up in the temple with Eli. Hannah's faith in God was clearly evident, as she literally gave up her child to God willingly. She truly "let go and let God."

Letting Go and Letting God Demands Faith

Letting go and letting God always demands that we exercise faith. You and I may not have to surrender the "right" to raise our children in our homes. We may not, as Hannah, have to be physically separated from them when they are small children. But we must be willing to commit them fully to the Lord—allowing him to have his will and his way in their lives for their entire existence. I believe this commitment should come even before the child is born.

Our two children were God's special gifts to my husband and me. He created them and gave them to us to care for and nurture for a few short years. We had to be willing to allow God to work in them as he desired, without our interference. It would involve giving up some of our plans, our hopes, and our dreams for them. It was, for us, a matter of surrender and obedience, bolstered by our faith in the omnipotent, omniscient, omnipresent Lord. We knew that one day, when the time was right, we would be called on to untie those apron strings and literally "let them go."

Walking by Faith

Second Corinthians 5:7 tells us that we "walk by faith, not by sight" (NASB). Often it is much easier to walk by sight than to walk by faith, especially where our children are concerned. And yet, Paul admonishes us in Colossians 2:6–7: "Therefore [as you] have received Christ Jesus the Lord, so walk in Him, having been firmly rooted and now being built up in Him and established in your faith, just as you were instructed" (NASB). Once we have received Jesus Christ by faith, we are to walk—to live—by faith. We have entrusted our lives to Jesus at salvation. Now, as born-again ones, we are to trust him with our daily lives and the lives of our offspring. We have embarked upon a "faith walk."

The Two Sides of Faith

Hebrews 11:6 says: "But without faith it is impossible to please him" (KJV). Years ago I heard Barbara Lee Johnson, a Christian women's speaker from Orlando, Florida, say that faith has two sides: "letting go" and "hanging on." At first that statement sounded contradictory, but the more I pondered it, the more I came to realize its truthfulness. Sometimes as I sought to exercise my faith and trust in God concerning my children, he showed me that I must let go of some things in my heart and life before I could pray in faith, believing. At other times, trusting God with my children meant hanging on to his promises as I waited for him to do his work in them. That also involved surrender—I had to yield to God's timetable for answering my prayers.

Letting Go of My Will

Frequently throughout my years of praying for my children I had to let go of something to which I was "holding on." Often it was my *desires* for my child. I might try to kid myself that I was really trusting God with my children, but until I let go of what *I* thought was best, I knew I was not truly entrusting them to God's care. I was making demands instead of requests. I was really saying, "Please, God, have *my* will, not yours."

I remember vividly when my daughter was in the eighth grade. She came home from school one afternoon and announced that she wanted to be on the basketball team. For some mothers that would not be a problem. For me, it was. You see, I had other plans for my daughter. I wanted her to follow in my footsteps, playing the piano and enjoying the school and church activities I had enjoyed. My vision for her did not include participation in organized sports. Since I was not one bit athletic, I simply did not appreciate sports programs for girls. Of course, I had already seen that Melanie was quite an athlete. She loved to play basketball whenever she could find a basketball goal.

I had hoped she had gotten any "athletic notions" out of her system. Was I ever wrong! When she wanted to play junior high basketball, her momma was not too thrilled. What was I going to tell her?

Wouldn't you know that as my husband and I prayed, God led us to a conference on the family! Dr. Howard Hendricks was one of the speakers. His theme was "Train up a child in the way he should go" from Proverbs 22:6 (KJV). Quite unexpectedly, I heard him say that to train up a child in the way he should go not only meant to encourage him in the way God intended him to go, but also in the way the child was bent. God had created our children with unique abilities and talents. They ought to be encouraged in that direction.[1] My conclusion: if our daughters were athletic and wanted to play ball, we ought to allow them to do so. If our sons were interested in writing, we ought to encourage them in that direction.

As I sat in our church sanctuary listening to Dr. Hendricks, the Holy Spirit spoke to my heart. I knew I must respond to his urgings. *Okay, Lord, I hear you,* was my silent reply to my heavenly Father that day. *I let go of my will for Melanie, my plans and desires for her, and I submit to your perfect will for her life. I know she is a super athlete and that you made her that way. I must allow her to use and develop those abilities you have equipped her with. I let go—but could I ask just one little thing, Lord? Could you please let her be feminine?!*

Melanie played junior high basketball for the next two years, moving on to her Christian high school varsity girls' basketball team when the junior high years were completed. My husband and I attended nearly every one of her games. We thoroughly enjoyed being spectators. When Melanie was a senior, she was point

122

guard for her team and played most of each game. Imagine my delight when during one of her senior year games, someone sitting behind us in the bleachers leaned over, tapped me on the shoulder, and exclaimed: "Sarah, just look at that Melanie. She could go to a wedding from the basketball court! She always has every hair in place." At that moment I realized that in yielding to God's will for Melanie, she and I had both been given the desires of our hearts: she was getting to play her beloved basketball, but she was a very feminine young lady! (Isn't God good!)

Today our daughter is a wonderful wife and mother of two, an outstanding women's speaker and Bible teacher, an excellent schoolteacher, and a gracious hostess. We are so very, very proud of her. She is everything we could want our daughter to be. Our God does such a wonderful job with our children when we "let them go" and let him have *his* way in their lives. He always does what is best for our children!

Letting Go of Fears and Fretting

As our two kids were maturing, it was not only my *plans* that I sometimes had to give up. In dealing with circumstances in each child's life, I frequently had to let go of my *fears*. I often was filled with fear for my children's well-being—with fear instead of faith. I wonder how many times I had to be reminded that I must let go of my fears if I was to walk by faith. How often did I hold on to those fears when I knew I should confess them and let them go?

At other times I had to let go of my fretting. In the July 4 devotional reading of *My Utmost for His Highest,* Oswald Chambers speaks to the issue of fretting. He states: "Fretting is one of God's great 'don'ts.' Fretting means getting ourselves 'out of joint' mentally or spiritually. Fretting rises from our determination to have our own way."[2]

God said: *"Do not fret—it leads only to evil"* (Ps. 37:8 NIV). One day he really convicted me of the sin of fretting, and I'll never forget what he taught me. That morning I was sitting at my desk, attempting to write an article for a magazine. Nothing would materialize. Why? Because I was fretting about the circumstances that had occurred in _____'s life. I was thinking: *If only this had not happened. If only that had not happened. If only, if only, if only.* I was living in the "circle of regret." My thoughts seemed to be circling around each other. I was getting absolutely nowhere. When we live in the "circle of regret," we are like a broken record, spinning round and round with an uncertain sound, making some very annoying noises, and being of use to no one.

Since I was not making progress with my writing, I decided to call for an appointment at the beauty shop. Perhaps a new hairdo would be the antidote for "what ailed me" (one of my grandmother's favorite descriptions). Fortunately, my beautician had time on her schedule.

The beautifying process entailed washing, setting, and sitting under the hairdryer for an hour. This lengthy stay under the dryer allowed ample time for reading and study. Since I had brought nothing to read, it didn't take long for me to resume my fretting and worrying. A lady came over to me to ask me if I had read a new book by Marjorie Holmes entitled *Lord, Let Me Love.* Since I had not, she offered it to me for my perusal. In my agitated state, I quickly flipped the pages. Nothing seemed to catch my attention until I turned a page and read the title: "If Only." The first sentence of the dissertation seemed to jump off the page. It read: "Please rescue me, God, from the 'if onlys.'"[3] Immediately I knew I had found the antidote. I needed to be "rescued" from the "if onlys." I was wallowing in the sin of unbelief.

I could hardly wait to get home to my place of prayer—a spot by the window in my living room. As I knelt there, I confessed to the Lord my sin of unbelief. You see, in reality I had been saying, "Lord, I don't believe you are big enough to handle this situation by yourself. I think I can help you by worrying." How foolish our human reasoning can be!

But the Lord did not chide me for that foolishness and lack of faith. Instead, he seemed to say to me that day, "I forgive you, and I want you to move from 'if only' to 'only God.' Only I (God) could have allowed this to happen to your child, for everything that comes into the life of the Christian is 'Father-filtered,' and only I (God) have the solution. Turn this situation over to me so that I can handle it for your child."

That morning I did move from "if only" to "only God" as I let go of my fretting and yielded this unpleasant predicament to my heavenly Father. I knew that God had allowed these circumstances and only *he* could solve this problem. I must "let go and let God." What was the result? God did work his perfect solution in that situation—a solution far better than I could have possibly imagined!

I cannot tell you how many times since that day I have had to repeat the process of moving from "if only" to "only God." God wants to rescue us from the "if onlys." He does not want us to spend our lives in the "circle of regret." When we find ourselves there, we can know that we are not walking by faith. We are not trusting God to take care of the situation. We are still trying to fix things ourselves. Something in our lives is unsurrendered. We must let go, moving from "if only" to "only God." As author Kay Arthur has said: "He knows how to extract maximum good and maximum glory out of every situation, no matter what."[4]

The Transition Years

As the years progressed, all too soon the transition period in our children's lives was upon us. The day when they would be "leaving the nest" loomed precariously on the horizon. One day I heard a presentation on the life of a mother eagle. I discovered that we mothers can learn a lot from observing the habits of the mother eagle. Listen to a passage from the book of Deuteronomy. In describing the greatness of our God, the writer of Deuteronomy compares Almighty God to an eagle and says: "Like an eagle that stirs up its nest and hovers over its young, that spreads its wings to catch them and carries them on its pinions. The LORD alone led him" (Deut. 32:11–12 NIV).

Matthew Henry, in his commentary on verse 11, gives us a clear picture of the eagle's ongoing relationship with her young. He points out that she protects them, makes provision for them, educates them, and teaches them to fly. Later on she "stirs them out of their nests where they lie dozing, flutters over them to show them how they must use their wings, and then accustoms them to fly upon her wings till they have learnt to fly on their own."[5] While the eaglets are learning to fly solo, just when they are about to fall to the ground, the mother eagle sweeps under them and carries them back to the starting place.[6]

As mothers, we make provision for our young children, educating them in morals and scriptural values and principles. The child-raising years are a time of fluttering over them. Like the mother eagle, we carry them "on our wings" many times as they depend on us for many things. We are there to pick them up when they fall, to serve as a sounding board for their complaints, and to be a listening ear and soft shoulder for their hurts. "Momma" is the one to whom they go so often—the one on whom they lean throughout their growing up years. But it is also our responsibility to teach them how to use their "wings." We know there will come a time when they must know how to "fly" by themselves. They cannot stay in the "nest" forever.

As we come closer to the time of "flying solo," the parent-child relationship will experience some changes. Just as the mother eagle stirs her eaglets out of the nest, we must encourage our children to "try their wings" more and more. This means that we must let go of some of the control of their lives, allowing them to make more decisions for themselves. Learning to "fly on your own" is not easy. We may have to sit back sometimes and watch our children be uncomfortable. It is an *unsettled* time for our children; it will often be *unsettling* for us.

While going through this difficult process, it helps to keep in mind the long-term goals for our children toward which we have been striving through the years. One goal is for them to be able to function well independently of us, both physically and emotionally. We want them to be dedicated fully to the Lord and submissive to his perfect will for their lives. What they need from us at this time is respect for their desire for

127

independence, encouragement in the right direction, and our constant prayer support. We must not seek to manipulate their lives; rather, we should seek to minister to them.

As my husband and I were traveling through this unpredictable transition time in our family, seeking to find a way to handle it gracefully, God led me to a book entitled *When Your Kids Aren't Kids Anymore,* by Jerry and Mary White. Authored by parents of four adult children, I knew it would contain helpful advice for mothers in the midst of this stage of their lives. (It was so insightful that I later taught the book in the women's ministry of our church.) The author stated that the elements of the parental process "can be summed up in four words: control, coaching, counsel and caring."[7] They described in detail each of these four elements. In doing so, they helped me to see that as the years advanced, my hands-on parenting was to slowly retreat. I was to move from the controlling and coaching phases into the counseling phase. The caring phase, however, which had begun before our children were born, would continue forever.

Verbal Restraint: The Order of the Day

While attending a party with several other mothers of soon-to-be-adult children, I heard a comment that aided me in the area of communication. One of the mothers told us of some counsel she had been given concerning her nearly adult children. "At this age," she had been advised, "they don't want you to ask them anything or tell them anything." I knew this was a nearly impossible task, but it really started me thinking. Didn't I need to ask fewer questions and give fewer instructions? Yes, I determined, I did. My new resolve was soon put into practice. Verbal restraint became my motto. I wasn't always successful, but my children will tell you that things improved.

I also learned that when we are communicating with these late-teenage children, our words are affected by the family's past history. We may be saying one thing, but our children may be "hearing" another because of past experiences. We must think and pray before we speak. Verbal restraint needs to be the order of the day. Our daily prayer should be: "Lord, fill my mouth with worthwhile stuff and nudge me when I've said enough."[8]

The Arrival of Adulthood

All too soon our first child reached adulthood. A few years later, our second child followed in her footsteps. We had entered a new season of our lives, with changes in our relationships. When something was "broken" in their lives, it was not Roland's or my responsibility to "fix" it. We were to be available for counsel and to spend much time in intercessory prayer on their behalf, but to "fix" it—no way! Joyce Rogers, in her excellent book *The Secret of a Woman's Influence,* gives some good advice about our relationship with our adult children. She says that our motto should be:

> Hands off, prayers on.
> Mouths shut, hearts open.[9]

As our children reach adulthood, we literally must "let them go." But in doing so, a new chapter will be opened for the majority of us—a chapter of relating to our children adult to adult. It will be a joyful time of shared experiences and blessings. As I stated in *A Woman's Garden of Prayer:* "This new relationship of adult to adult can be so precious, as you see that child of yours growing up and assuming responsibilities, as you see him put into practice those many things he's learned 'at mother's knee.'"[10] And don't ever forget: "Those adult children will still need your love, your support, your counsel and your prayers. You are and always will be their *mother*."[11]

In every phase of our children's lives, we are called on to "let go and let God"—to submit to his will and his way for our children. When the time comes for them to be on their own, we must "untie those apron strings"—truly letting go of our children. At the same time, we must hang on to God and his precious promises. As we intercede for our children, you and I can trust God to hear and answer our prayers, to work mightily in their lives, and to make all things that happen to them work together for their good and his glory. God is in control. He is sovereign, and he is utterly trustworthy! God says in Jeremiah 33:3: "Call to Me and I will answer you, and I will tell you great and mighty things, which you do not know" (NASB). In Psalm 138:8 we gain further assurance from our Lord: "The LORD will perfect that which concerns me" (NKJV).

A young man had a plaque on his bedroom wall that read: "Let God!" As he was striving to let God have his way in his life, the young man seemed to be getting nowhere. One day when he came into his room, he noticed something different about this plaque. The *d* had fallen off. The plaque no longer read, "Let God." It now read: "Let Go."

At that moment the light seemed to dawn for the young man. He realized there was something he needed to do. In order to let God have his perfect way in his life, he needed to let go of some things to which he was holding on. Until he "let go and let God," he could not accomplish God's purposes for him. He must surrender to the Lord.

Roland and I let go and let God have his way in our children's lives.

Conclusion: Looking Back/Looking Forward

Looking Back

Yes, dear young women, in answer to your question "If you could go back in time, what would you do differently in your child raising?" there are many things I would probably change. There are many things I would *not* change. In this book I have listed only ten. I could not possibly enumerate them all.

BUT GOD! God is faithful, and he heard and answered my prayers: *prayers of confession,* when I didn't handle situations as he would have desired, when I made errors in judgment and decisions not pleasing to him, when I failed to be the mother he so desired me to be. He heard my *prayers of petition and intercession* for my children—for their needs to be met, for them to walk in his ways and his truth, for their mates, their missions, and their ministries. God heard my *requests for wisdom and discernment.* He heard my *cries of desperation,* when I did not know how or what to pray. God always prompted me never to give up on him or on my children. No matter how much time I spent in "God's Waiting Room," I knew he would answer my prayers in his own way, in his own time.

Today, as I stand looking back down the highway of my life, one of the greatest lessons I have learned is this: No matter how many times we fail, God will never fail us or forsake us or forget us. Nor will he fail or forsake or forget our children. With that assurance, we can stand firmly on his promises—"For no matter how many promises God has made, they are 'Yes' in Christ" (2 Cor. 1:20 NIV). We can stand in complete confidence upon his Holy Word—his Word is absolutely trustworthy and absolutely true. We can trust him with our children. He will take our messes and "unmess" them. In answer to our prayers, he will take our failures and turn them into victories. He will take our shortcomings and use them to build character in our children's lives (see Rom. 8:28).

Always remember: There is nothing too hard for the Lord. Jeremiah 32:17 states it best: "Ah, Sovereign LORD, you have made the heavens and the earth by your great power and outstretched arm. Nothing is too hard for you" (NIV).

Never give up on your children!
Never give up on God!

Looking Forward

As we look toward the future, we must not forget the lessons of the past. Josh McDowell, internationally known leader of youth, states:

Once upon a time, children were raised in an atmosphere that communicated absolute standards for behavior: certain things were right and certain things were

133

wrong. A child's parents, teachers, ministers, youth workers, and other adults collaborated in an effort to communicate that the former should be heeded and the latter should be avoided. At one time, our society, by and large, explained the universe, humanity, and the purpose of life from the Judeo-Christian tradition: a belief that truth existed, and everyone could know and understand it. . . . That has changed drastically, however. Our children are being raised in a society that has largely rejected the notions of truth and morality, a society that has somewhere lost the ability to decide what is true and what is right. Truth has become a matter of 'taste; morality has been replaced by individual preference.' . . . It is painfully apparent that many of our kids have lost the ability to distinguish between right and wrong.[1]

The time in which society viewed the world from a Judeo-Christian perspective was indeed the time in which my husband and I were being raised. It was the *Leave It to Beaver* fifties—a peaceful and uncomplicated time in which to grow up. Even those who did not embrace our Christian beliefs operated from a platform of morality based on the Judeo-Christian ethic. They might not do what was right, but they knew the difference between right and wrong.

We watched sadly as this viewpoint drastically changed in the sixties, seventies, and eighties. God was dethroned. Man was enthroned. Secular humanism invaded—and eventually pervaded—every facet of our society. This upheaval occurred in our schools, in the media, in government, on the public square. Prayer and Bible reading were removed from the public schools. Abortion was legalized. A sexual revolution broke out across our land. "What God says" was replaced by "What man thinks."

To watch what was happening was disconcerting to me. God called me to enter the public arena. I became involved not only in taking a strong stand for righteousness but also in seeking to disseminate Christian values in our city, state, and nation. I quickly discovered that I had entered a battleground! The public schools and the media were among the first to be secularized. We Christians found it hard to get across our message. The textbooks no longer voiced our beliefs; the schools became more and more closed to Christian witness. The media was controlled by secular humanists who promoted their secular humanistic viewpoints in show after show, hour after hour, day after day. The Christian viewpoint was rarely espoused through the media.

As we reflect on our world today, realizing what has happened in our society, does it not behoove us to commit to restoring these foundational beliefs of morality and truth? If we cannot do anything else, we can teach these truths at home!

Remember James Dobson's words: "Most American children receive no spiritual training whatsoever!"[2] With the uncertainties of the future looming before us, is there not a desperate call to parents to fulfill their God-given responsibilities of motherhood and fatherhood? It is the parents who have the primary responsibility for raising their children *"in the instruction and training of the Lord."* "Yet most American children receive no spiritual training whatsoever!"[3] Parents— who have been given these special treasures from the

Lord—must mold and shape them in such a way that they will be godly adults. "Yet most American children receive no spiritual training whatsoever!"[4]

Are you preparing your children to live in the world they must inhabit? Will they be able to stand alone in the face of peer pressure and worldly entice-ments? Will they be "G-rated" kids in an "R-rated" world?

Perhaps you are asking, "Is there a secret to raising 'G-rated' kids in an 'R-rated' world?" This book has addressed many issues involved in answering this question. While no one has all the answers, perhaps these words in summation will be beneficial.

When asked the secret of raising "G-rated" kids in an "R-rated" world, Christian counselor and mother Pat Brand answered: "Parents must be ready to dispel the attraction of the 'R-rated' world. They must know the enemy in order to battle it. They also must stay so contemporary, their children will believe they know what they are talking about."[5] Parents also must be so trustworthy that their kids will know they can trust them! That doesn't mean you will always be right. But when you are not, you must admit it and ask forgive-ness. Acknowledge misunderstandings. Be honest and real with them.

It is important to know what is happening in your children's lives. Don't be afraid to ask them questions. Filter everything (including friends, dress, language, music, activities) through the principles of God's Word. Make the Bible the standard for your life and theirs.

Perhaps the best advice I heard about raising "G-rated" kids in an "R-rated" world came from a mother of five. She said: "The secret to raising

'G-rated' kids in an 'R-rated' world is to remember the word *grace*. It is God's grace that continues to surround us and our family. We can do our part to raise 'G-rated' children, but we will make mistakes. Our God by his grace, can take even our mistakes and work them for his good and glory [see Rom. 8:28]. To have 'G-rated' kids, we need to love God more, pray more, trust him more, praise him more, worship him, and keep our focus on him."[6]

The prayer in John 17:15 is the prayer we need to pray for our children: "I do not pray that You should take them out of the world, but that You should keep them from the evil one" (NKJV). Only God can enable them to be godly in an ungodly world. But God is able! He can do "exceeding abundantly above all that we ask or think, according to the power that worketh in us" (Eph. 3:20 KJV). Praise his Name! Nothing is too hard for the Lord!

APPENDIX A

How to Pray for Your Children

For many years I used the following outline to pray for my children.

1. PRAY FOR YOUR CHILD'S *DECISION* TO FOLLOW JESUS CHRIST AS SAVIOR AND LORD

Romans 3:23: "For all have sinned and fall short of the glory of God." (NIV)

Romans 10:9–10: "That if you confess with your mouth, 'Jesus is Lord,' and believe in your heart that God raised him from the dead, you will be saved. For it is with your heart that you believe and are justified, and it is with your mouth that you confess and are saved." (NIV)

Your child's decision to follow Jesus Christ as Savior and Lord is the most important decision he or she will ever make. I believe we as parents should pray that our children will come to know Jesus as Savior and Lord as early as possible. What a blessing it will be for them to serve him all their lives.

I know it can be a problem for parents to know when their little ones are old enough to understand the meaning of salvation. I remember well our own situation with our son Alan. When Alan was six years old, he began to ask us if he could give his heart to

Jesus. We were thrilled, but also a bit apprehensive, wanting to be certain he understood what he was doing. We put him off for several weeks.

One Sunday night, just after we had gotten in bed and turned off the lights, Alan came into our bedroom and handed us a handwritten letter. Roland quickly sat up, turned on the light, and read his letter aloud. It said:

Dear Jesus,

I want to be saved, but my parents won't let me.

Love,

Alan

Needless to say, we got out of our beds and went into Alan's room. After Roland explained why we had put off this decision, he discussed with Alan the meaning of salvation. Convinced that our son knew what he was doing, we all knelt by his bed. That night Alan gave his heart to Jesus Christ, just as I, too, had given my heart to Jesus at six years of age many years previously in Crystal Springs, Mississippi. It was a joyous night at our house!

Since many children will not make this commitment to Jesus Christ at an early age, we need to commit to praying for as long as it takes for them to respond to the gospel. We must not get discouraged and give up. We must keep on praying until the answer comes!

2. PRAY FOR YOUR CHILD TO BE *DELIVERED* FROM EVIL

Matthew 6:13: "And lead us not into temptation, but deliver us from the evil one." (NIV)

John 17:15: "I do not pray that You
should take them out of the world, but that
You should keep them from the evil one."
(NKJV)

2 Thessalonians 3:2–3: "And pray that
we may be delivered from wicked and evil
men. . . . But the Lord is faithful, and he will
strengthen and protect you from the evil
one." (NIV)

To pray for our children to be delivered from evil
and the evil one is perhaps as important in today's
world as it has ever been. How important it is for us to
ask our heavenly Father to protect our children every
moment of their lives!

The prayer I often pray for my children is as
follows:

Lord God, Jehovah, in the name of
the Lord Jesus Christ and in the power of
the blood of the Lord Jesus Christ, I stand
against Satan in _____'s life.
I ask you to place a hedge of protection
around him and a hedge of thorns. I pray
that you will "establish [his] footsteps in
Your Word, and do not let any iniquity have
dominion over [him]." [from Ps. 119:133
NASB] In Jesus' name I pray, amen.

3. PRAY THAT YOUR CHILD WILL LEAD A *DISCIPLINED* LIFE

Proverbs 16:32: "He who is slow to anger
is better than the mighty, and he who rules
his spirit than he who takes a city." (NKJV)

To lead a disciplined life one must learn self-
discipline. He must learn to be "slow to anger" as well

as "to rule his spirit." An important element of a disciplined life is making good use of one's time. Oh, how
our children need to set these positive goals for their
lives! It has been said that being disciplined means
being able to say no to self and yes to God. It is vital
that we pray for our children to lead disciplined lives.

4. PRAY FOR YOUR CHILD TO HAVE DISCRETION

Ephesians 3:14, 16: "For this reason I bow
my knees before the Father . . . that He
would grant you, according to the riches of
His glory, to be strengthened with power
through His Spirit in the inner man." (NASB)

Surely we want our children to be discreet.
Discretion is defined in the dictionary as "discernment which enables a person to judge critically what
is correct and proper, united with caution."[1] In this
"anything goes" society, how essential it is for the
Christian young person to have discretion and good
judgment, united with caution. Today, as the world
seems to have "thrown caution to the wind," such
should not be the case for us as Christians.

We need to pray Ephesians 3:16 for our children—
that they "be strengthened with might by his Spirit in
the inner man" (KJV). William Barclay comments on
verse sixteen in this way: "By 'the inner man' the
Greeks understood three things: (1) There was man's
reason. (2) There was the conscience. (3) There was
the will."[2] He goes on to comment: "It was Paul's
prayer that Christ should strengthen the reasoning
power of his friends. He wanted them to be better able
to discern between that which was right and that
which was wrong. He wanted them to be less at the

mercy of their passions, and their instincts, and their desires. He wanted Christ to give them the wisdom which would keep life pure and safe."[3]

Following Barclay's ideas, as I divide the inner man into three areas—mind, emotions, and will—I like to pray this prayer:

Lord God, I pray for my child in the area of his *mind,* that he will be able to discern between good and evil and between better and best.

I pray for my child in the area of his *emotions,* that he will not be at the mercy of his instincts, passions and desires, but will be sensitive to the leading of the Holy Spirit.

I pray for my child in the area of his *will,* that when he knows what to do, he will do it; when he knows what not to do, he will not do it.

5. PRAY THAT YOUR CHILD WILL BE *DILIGENT*

Colossians 3:23: "Whatever you do, do your work heartily, as for the Lord rather than for men." (NASB)

Psalm 37:5: "Commit your way to the LORD, trust also in Him, and He will do it." (NASB)

Psalm 37:23–24: "The steps of a man are established by the LORD, and He delights in his way. When he falls, he will not be hurled headlong, because the LORD is the One who holds his hand." (NASB)

Diligence is "the constant and earnest effort to accomplish what is undertaken." One who is diligent is "industrious and persevering."[4] *We live in a day of casual commitment; but God demands our full and total commitment.* Our children need to learn the meaning of commitment. They need to learn to finish what they start. They need to give constant and earnest effort to the work they undertake. God wants us to live for him and not for ourselves. Nor does he want our lives compartmentalized with the secular in one box and the sacred in another. Everything we do "in word or deed, do it all in the name of the Lord Jesus, giving thanks to God the Father through him" (Col. 3:17 NIV). In Ephesians 6:7, we read: "Serve wholeheartedly, as if you were serving the Lord, not men, because you know that the Lord will reward everyone for whatever good he does" (NIV). If our children can learn these principles as young men and women, it will make a tremendous difference in their attitudes and performances.

6. PRAY FOR YOUR CHILD TO *DISCOVER* THE WILL OF GOD FOR HIS LIFE

Psalm 32:8: "I will instruct you and teach you in the way which you should go; I will counsel you with My eye upon you." (NASB)

Jeremiah 29:11: "'For I know the plans that I have for you,' declares the LORD, 'plans for welfare and not for calamity to give you a future and a hope.'" (NASB)

Colossians 4:12: "Always laboring earnestly for you in his prayers, that you may stand perfect and fully assured in all the will of God." (NASB)

Colossians 1:9: "For this reason also, since the day we heard of it, we have not ceased

to pray for you and to ask that you may be
filled with the knowledge of His will in all
spiritual wisdom and understanding." (NASB)
Ephesians 5:17: So then do not be foolish, but understand what the will of the
Lord is." (NASB)

We should pray earnestly and continuously for
our children to "stand perfect and fully assured in all
the will of God." This includes discovering God's will
concerning their mission, their mate, and their ministry. Because choices, both great and small, have significance, we need to pray for their daily decisions.

The secularist world will tell our children to look
within for the answers. We must pray that they look to
the *Lord* for his guidance and leadership in their lives—
that they will daily seek his will, not just in the big
things, but also in the small and mundane. Ephesians
5:17 is a warning to all: "So then do not be foolish, but
understand what the will of the Lord is" (NASB).

Other petitions should include: (1) that our kids
understand early the folly of following their own
devices—the foolishness of "doing their own thing";
(2) that they realize God has a wonderful plan for their
lives and that true happiness comes only when they
are walking according to his plan; (3) that God is concerned about every detail of their lives—he created
them, he loves them, he will care for them. Praise his
holy Name!

7. PRAY THAT YOUR CHILD WILL BE FULLY *DEDICATED* TO THE LORD

Matthew 22:37: "Jesus replied: 'Love the
Lord your God with all your heart and with
all your soul and with all your mind.'" (NIV)

That our children be godly young men and women should be our preeminent prayer for them. This will happen only as they dedicate themselves fully to the Lord. To *dedicate* means "to give wholly or chiefly to a person or purpose."[5] For the Christian, that *person* is Jesus Christ and that *purpose* is to glorify him. We must pray that our kids will give themselves wholly and completely to Jesus Christ for the purpose of glorifying him in every aspect of their lives. If we have taught them that God is the source of their strength, that he is utterly trustworthy, that he will never leave them or forsake them, how much easier it will be for them to dedicate their lives to him.

Let us intercede daily for our children!

Note: In 1999, along with Patti Webb, I co-authored a book on praying for one's children called *A Mother's Garden of Prayer*. You can find it at Christian bookstores and on the Internet. It is a guide to praying Scripture for your children, from the pre-born child through adulthood. It contains more than fifty circumstances when a mother and grandmother need to pray for their children and grandchildren. It will help you to pray for your child according to God's Word.

APPENDIX B

Enjoying Your Teenagers

(Adapted from a seminar by Pat Brand titled "Enjoying Your Teenagers." Revised and additions by author. Used by permission.)

Pat Brand introduced her conference on teenagers by saying: "There are many challenges one could desire to accomplish in this life—rowing a boat upstream on the Mississippi River, running a small third-world country, or dedicating your life to becoming the next winner of the Nobel Peace Prize. These are all noble endeavors, but certainly one of the most challenging of all pursuits is to 'enjoy' your teenagers.

"They don't make it easy for their parents. They are busily breaking away from parental authority. Much of the time it seems as if they don't want their parents around anymore. If you are the parent of a teenager, don't think there is something wrong with you. There is nothing wrong with you. There is nothing wrong with them. This is the time when they are supposed to begin exercising some independence. The problem becomes: How will we let them learn independence without it 'robbing us' of our joy?

"Parents are given much advice on the teenage years. As one father said: The only people not having trouble with their teenagers are people who don't have any. "Raising a teenager is not easy. It takes work, patience, and dedication. The rewards, however, are great. The thing you must remember is this: You are not alone. There are many, many others who are at this very moment walking in your shoes."

Mrs. Brand then divided the tasks of parenting a teenager into three main categories: Education, Edification, and Endurance.

Education. The word *educate* means "to develop the faculties and powers of [a person] by teaching, instruction, or schooling."[1] By the time your children reach thirteen, they have already had much education, both formal and informal. In the area of formal education, they have learned academics, have been engaged in sports, have had some contact with the arts/humanities, and hopefully, have had good Christian training. Their informal education has taken place everywhere they have gone—at school, at church, in the community, and most of all, at home.

As parents, we play a vital role in their education. We are constantly teaching them things by example. From us they learn attitudes, prejudices, routines, and traditions. The attitudes we have about what goes on in school, in the work place, and at home are the very same attitudes our children will adopt. They learn much from observing our actions and reactions. It would be a beneficial exercise to periodically ask ourselves: *What are my children learning from my outlook on life? From my lifestyle? What are they learning from me about priorities, the things that are most important in life?*

One of the most important aspects of informal learning for teens is in the realm of peer pressure. Peer pressure raises its ugly head in five major areas: (1) music, (2) driving, (3) appearance, (4) sex, and

(5) rules. Two important thoughts should be addressed first. It is essential to remember that as parents we are greatly influenced by our peers too. We dress like our friends, go to the same places they go, avoid the places they avoid, and adhere to similar rules of living. Recognizing this should help parents be more aware of the amount of pressure our kids are encountering and the stresses they have to withstand each day. Secondly, if your family has practiced "open communication" with your kids, you have "a thirteen-year head start" on the families with communication problems. Keeping the lines of communication open is a constant challenge but an essential ingredient of effective parenting during the teenage years.

The area of Christian education is an integral part of the teenager's life. Since peers are so important at this time, church-based activities and programs become even more vital. (The benefits of church attendance have already been addressed in this book. The parent's responsibility in spiritual development has been discussed at length. But there is something that must be inserted at this point: As a parent, you need to make certain that your teenagers have come to a saving knowledge of Jesus Christ; believe in the inerrant, infallible Word of God; know what they believe; and know why they believe it. It is never too late to be concerned about these four things. What they believe will affect the choices they make and the lives they live in the future.) We parents are responsible for our children's Christian education.

Edification. The second area where parents are important in their teenagers' lives is in the area of edification. To *edify* means "to build up." Ephesians 4:29 says: "Do not let any unwholesome talk come out of your mouths, but only what is helpful for building others up [edifying] according to their needs" (NIV).

Edifying—building up—your child begins with accepting him as God created him, not trying to make the child into your own or someone else's concept of what he should be. There are three areas on which to focus: concern, cost, and commitment.

Concern. We are all concerned about our children. "That concern can be manifested through critical words or caring words." Because of our concern, we may use criticism and sarcasm, or find ourselves constantly nagging the child. God has much to say in his Holy Word about sarcasm and nagging (see Eph. 6:4; Prov. 27:15; Prov. 21:19 as examples). Think of the phrases parents of teenagers most often use with their kids: Pick up your clothes; Turn down that TV, radio, CD player; Get off that phone; Help your sister/brother; Have you finished your homework? ; Did you wash your hands?; Where are you going?; Drive carefully; Why didn't you tell me? You need a haircut; etc. "These things may need to be stated or asked, but they should not be the sum total of all conversations we have with our children. We should be about the job of nurturing and caring. Caring manifests itself altogether differently."

How can we show our teenagers how much we care? There are at least six components to caring: (1) touching, (2) time, (3) listening, (4) laughter, (5) tears, and (6) compliments.

Caring is touching. Touches are important. Hugs and kisses should be given as often as the kids will allow. A Christian psychologist gave some really good advice: Because teenagers sometimes resist hugs and kisses, try giving them little pats whenever possible. It is one way to "keep in touch."

Caring is time. Many of today's parents try to rationalize about "quality" time spent with their kids. All the time your children spend with you should be *quality* time. However, kids need to spend both *quality* time and *quantity* time with their parents. You cannot give encouragement and approval without a lot of time and expenditure. Of course parents are busy these days; most families are two-income families. This presents great challenges to finding family time. Nonetheless, we must remember the order in which God wants us to prioritize our lives: God first, our mate second, our children third, and all else fourth, fifth, etc.

"Since the time you get to spend with your teenager will be limited, even though he isn't always available when you need him, try to be available when he needs you. If you continually give your kids the idea that you are too busy for them, they will look for—and usually find—someone who is not too busy. That someone will not necessarily be a person of your choosing." Remember: those activities, projects, and fun events will be there for you to go back to; your son or daughter will never be this age again. He or she will be gone before you know it. Now is the time to be a caring parent. Be available to your kids.

Caring is listening. "This is the season of your life when you need to begin listening more than you talk. If you have a teenage daughter, you may have to listen to miles and miles of chatter before you hear one inch of a problem or concern." Stay up until she gets home from her dates. Make it easy for her to open up to you by listening without interrupting.

Proverbs 18:13 says: "He who answers before listening—that is his folly and his shame" (NIV). Monitor
carefully your reactions and responses to your
teenagers' comments. Remember the words of the
apostle James: "Everyone should be quick to listen,
slow to speak and slow to become angry, for man's
anger does not bring about the righteous life that
God desires" (James 1:19–20 NIV).

Caring is laughing with your child. Healthy families
have fun together. They laugh a lot. They love to tell
jokes and tease other family members. They like to
play tricks on each other. "Teens love amusement
parks, video games, goofy movies, and gutsy dads.
They love mothers who "fuss" at them for all their
silliness while still participating in their fun adventures. They are going to have fun—be sure some of it
is at home."

Caring is tears. "Relationships are critical to all
human beings. In the teenage years they are ultra-
critical." Creating new relationships is risky for the
teenager because he is so unsure of himself. The
breakup of relationships can bring many tears. Losing
at sports or academics can cause tears. Not being able
to look like the others, dress like the others, or go
places the others go—all are occasions for tears. "Our
job as parents is to comfort them in their sadness, not
to admonish or make light of their pain. What has
happened may seem silly and insignificant to you, but
it is vitally important to them. This is a time to keep
the proper perspective. Most teenagers cannot see life
beyond next Friday night's ballgame!"

Caring includes complimenting them. Teens are never
pleased with themselves, it seems. Listen to some
common complaints: I am too fat, too thin, too short,

too ugly. My hair looks awful, my skin is terrible, I don't speak well, my grades are poor. On and on they go. "They are one big bundle of insecurity. They don't need parents to confirm those facts. It behooves us, therefore, as parents to find something daily about which to compliment them. Undoubtedly, this will not be easy. They will tell you to stop. They will tell you that your compliments don't count because you are their parents and have to 'like' them. But in reality, they feed on those compliments more than they feed on pizza. Compliments to the teenager are as essential to their emotional health as protein and vitamin C are to their physical health."

Cost. The second part of the edification/encouragement of our children. It will cost us as parents: "our energy, our time, our money, and our prayers." One thing parents need to pray for is the stamina to keep up with their kids! The importance of spending time with your kids can never be overemphasized. "If it means sacrificing something you would rather do in order to put your kids' needs first, it will certainly be worth it." Remember: your kids need quality time and quantity time with their parents!

In the area of money, it goes without saying that it costs a lot of money to raise children. Of course they don't need all the things they want; your job is to seek to give them what they need. Their wants and needs are in two very different categories. It is always a problem to determine how to spend one's money wisely. "Sometimes the 'cost' to the parents is the animosity they receive from their kids when they refuse to indulge their every want."

In today's society there is a plethora of "child worship." Parents seem to be afraid not to give their kids what they want. We often see a son or daughter who is never satisfied and "suffers" from their parents' overindulgence. Parents are kept busy seeking to keep up with the world's standards of materialism. They spend so much time trying to give their children what they want instead of what they need that the parents are frazzled, worn out, and burned out. As a byproduct of this lifestyle, they end up giving their children "things" instead of spending the time to train them in the way they should go.

There is another danger inherent in this practice of child worship—much "giving" on the part of the parents with very little "receiving" from the child. Child expert Peggy Perkins says that the characteristic that concerns her most about parents in the twenty-first century is "their desire to give the child everything he wants to make him happy and failing to require much, if anything, from him—failing to teach the child to wait for and earn some of the things he desires."[2] The teenage years are an excellent time for them to learn that everything has a price tag.

Commitment. In order to edify our children—to build them up as God would have us do—there will be concern and caring, there is a cost we must pay, and above all, there must be a *commitment* to seeing them through this difficult time. "Sometimes *we* know we are committed to our children and *God* knows it, but the *kids* don't know it." They need to know of our unwavering commitment to them.

This brings us to prayer. We need to pray about every aspect of our teenagers' lives. This is a vital part of carrying out our commitment to them. It is as essential to their spiritual growth and development (and their emotional health) as is nutrition to their physical health. We need to pray for ourselves too. We need God's wisdom at this season of our lives. How grateful we should be that God's Word tells us that when we ask for wisdom, God will give us a liberal dose! As has already been stated in this book, for the Christian mother, prayer is a necessity: she can't do without it; her family can't do without it.

We must pray without ceasing—every day, and sometimes every hour. We must pray specific prayers—expecting specific answers. Prayer partners are a wonderful blessing at this season of your life. The love, support, and prayers of other prayer warriors will be invaluable in dealing with the daily challenges of teenagers. Praying *with* your teenager will be rewarding to both of you too. Pray with them as much as they will allow. Then you can pray privately for those areas in which you know they are hurting, but won't share.

Second, find out what your kids believe about God and the Bible. Have discussions with them on spiritual matters. Don't do all of the talking; listen carefully to what they are saying. If there are areas of confusion and uncertainty on their part, this is the time to establish what God's Word teaches. They need to settle their beliefs and determine their convictions before they leave home. In a short time they will be out on their own, facing monumental challenges. What they believe will affect the choices they make and the lives they live in the future.

Endurance. The third and final element of parenting teenagers is endurance. This will include "consistent, daily prayer" (which has already been discussed) and "a persistent godly example." It will include "keeping on keeping on," no matter the delight or drudgery of the day. It will entail seeking to keep the lines of communication open, no matter what happens in the child's life. What your child needs to know, perhaps more than anything else (besides knowing Jesus as his personal Lord and Savior) is that you love him unconditionally. He needs to know for certain that his mother and father will love him— always and forever.

In the area of example, you and I must live out Christianity if we want our children to learn it. If I want my child to read the Bible, he must see that Bible reading is very important in my life—that reading the Bible is as natural as reading a newspaper or magazine. If I want him to memorize Scripture, I must memorize it too (if I have not already done so). If I want him to love our church, my attitude and attendance must reflect my love for our church. In other words, we must attempt to "practice what we preach." Dr. Charles Stanley's quote (used earlier in this book) is apropos: "There is nothing under heaven like a mother and a father patterning principles they believe in if they want to hand those principles down to their children."[3]

Our goal is to move our children toward independence, ultimately working ourselves out of a job. We must not attempt to solve all our children's problems. They must be allowed to learn from their mistakes and to work out some of their dilemmas while they are still at home.

A major part of "enduring" your teenagers should be your refusal to give up on your children or on God's ability to work in their lives. Never give up on your child! Never give up on God! You may not see how God is working in their lives at this moment. You may not see the fruit of your labor today or tomorrow.

Nonetheless, just keep on asking, keep on seeking, and keep on knocking! (See Matt. 7). Nothing is too hard for the Lord!

Jeremiah 32:17 says: "Ah, Sovereign LORD, you have made the heavens and the earth by your great power and outstretched arm. Nothing is too hard for you" (NIV).

APPENDIX C

Drifting Away from God

It was our fervent desire that we as a family would keep growing spiritually throughout our lives. Spiritual growth is a continuous process that requires constant effort. This is true for every believer. If we are not growing, if we are not constantly making the effort to grow spiritually, we cannot expect to remain where we are. Like a boat that has been untied from the pier, we will begin to drift downstream away from our basic beliefs and convictions.

"Ten Steps to Drifting"

I'll never forget the teachings of a young man whose life greatly influenced our son. His name was Dan Dehaan. He met an untimely death in the prime of his ministry when the plane in which he was on hit the side of a mountain. Dan had shared with our young people what he entitled "Ten Steps to Drifting." In his book *Intercepted by Christ,* he speaks to the issue:

> What is drifting? It is taking the easy way out! It is slowly moving in the wrong direction. It is dying by degrees. The end is certain, but the way there may be ever so slow. Drifting usually begins with carelessness. We simply fail to pay attention and we get lazy.

This may lead to a curiosity for sin. When we are careless, we get curious, and if we fail to stop the pattern, we will have contact with sin. After the contact, we usually go to conniving and then we find ourselves living in carnality. From carelessness to curiosity—from curiosity to contact—from contact to conniving—from conniving to carnality. A study of David's fall into the sin of adultery and murder will show this progression. He became lazy, then curious. He decided to make contact with sin, then tried to connive his way out of it. Finally, he lost his desire for spiritual things.[1]

My husband and I prayed that our children would be insightful enough to recognize when they were drifting away from God and halt this dangerous process by turning back to the source of their strength. We knew, however, that in some instances, as in our own lives, God would have to allow some props to be removed—allow them to be uncomfortable—in order to bring them back to himself. That might mean that we would have to sit back and watch them in this undesirable condition. We must pray. We must wait. We must trust our God. Only he can restore spiritual wholeness.

Endnotes

CHAPTER 1

1. Gary Smalley and John Trent, *The Blessing* (Nashville, Tenn.: Thomas Nelson Inc., l986), 55, 59. All rights reserved.

2. Maxine Marsolini, *Blended Families: Creating Harmony as You Build a New Home Life* (Chicago, Ill.: Moody Publishers, 2000), 20. Used by permission.

3. Gary Smalley and John Trent, *The Gift of Honor* (Nashville, Tenn.: Thomas Nelson, Inc., 1987), 89. All rights reserved.

4. Charles Stanley, *How To Keep Your Kids on Your Team* (Nashville, Tenn.: Thomas Nelson, Inc., 1986), 108. All rights reserved.

5. Smalley and Trent, *The Blessing,* 93.

6. Ibid., 89.

7. Stanley, *How to Keep Your Kids on Your Team,* 105.

8. Vicki Mullins, a minister's wife and mother of two, author's questionnaire.

9. Smalley and Trent, *The Gift of Honor,* 17.

10. Patty Hankins, mother of three successful adult sons, author's questionnaire.

11. Smalley and Trent, *The Blessing,* 59.

12. Mullins, author's questionaire.

13. C. Van Snider, M.D., Associated Clinical Professor of Pediatrics at University of Tennessee Center of Health Sciences, Memphis, Tennessee, author's questionnaire.

14. Ibid.

CHAPTER 2

1. Author unknown.

2. Joe Batten, Wendy Havemann, Bill Pearce, and Gail Pedersen, *Tough-Minded Parenting* (Nashville, Tenn.: Broadman Press, 1991), 131.

3. William Makepeace Thackeray as quoted in *God's Little Devotional Book for Moms* (Tulsa, Okla.: Honor Books, 1995, 2001), 252.

4. Mullins, author's questionnaire.

5. St. Augustine, *Words of Life,* ed. Charles L. Walls (New York, NY: Harper and Row Publishers, 1966), 18.

6. Ruth Ann VanderSteeg, mother of five adult children, Lakeland, Tennessee, author's questionnaire.

7. Vicki Snider, author's questionnaire.

8. Eric Brand, businessman and father of four, author's questionnaire.

9. VanderSteeg, author's questionnaire.

10. Mullins, author's questionnaire.

11. Van Snider, M.D., author's questionnaire.

CHAPTER 3

1. E. J. Daniels, evangelist from Florida.

2. *The Women's Study Bible*: New King James Version, ed. Dorothy Kelly Patterson (Nashville, Tenn.: Thomas Nelson Publishers, 1995), 2067. Used by permission.

3. Ibid.

4. Patsy Clairmont, *God Uses Cracked Pots* (Colorado Springs, Colo.: Focus on the Family Publishing, 1991), 18.

CHAPTER 4

1. Told to author by her mother Mabel (Mrs. Joe T.) Riley Odle in Jackson, Mississippi.

2. James Dobson, *Bringing Up Boys* (Wheaton, Ill.: Tyndale House Publishers, Inc., 2001), 102. Used by permission.

3. VanderSteeg, author's questionnaire.

4. George Barna, *The Future of the American Family* (Chicago, Ill.: Moody Publishing, 1993), 107. Used by permission.

5. Arlene Skolnick and Jerome Skolnick, *Families in Transition,* 6th ed. (Glenview, Ill.: Scott, Foresman and Company, 1989). Taken from *The Future of the American Family* by George Barna.

6. Dobson, *Bringing Up Boys,* 102.

7. Leroy Brownlow, *A Psalm in My Heart* (Fort Worth, Tex.: Brownlow Publishing Co., 1989), May 2.

8. John Phillips, *Exploring the Psalms,* vol. 2 (Neptune, N.J.: Loizeau Brothers, 1986), 53. Used by permission.

CHAPTER 5

1. Benjamin Spock and Michael B. Rothenberg, *Dr. Spock's Baby and Child Care* (New York, N.Y.: Pocket Books, 1998).

2. Dr. James Dobson, *The Strong-Willed Child, Birth Through Adolescence* (Wheaton, Ill.: Tyndale House Publishers, Inc., 1978), 20. Used by permission.

3. Van Snider, M.D., author's questionnaire.

4. Dobson, *The Strong-Willed Child,* 76.

5. Ibid., 31–33.

6. Dobson, *Bringing Up Boys,* 236.

7. *Random House Dictionary of the English Language,* s.v. "discipline."

8. Mark Lee, *Our Children Are Our Best Friends* (Grand Rapids, Mich.: Zondervan Publishing House, 1970), 178.

9. William T. Slonecker, M.D., *Parenting Principles from the Heart of a Pediatrician* (Nashville: Broadman & Holman, 2003), 68.

10. Author unknown.

11. Lee, *Our Children Are Our Best Friends,* 162.

12. *Random House Dictionary of the English Language,* s.v. "teach."

13. Ibid., s.v. "train."

14. Charles Thompson, Ph.D., professor of educational psychology and counseling at the University of Tennessee, Knoxville. Used by permission.

15. Dr. Adrian Rogers, sermon at Bellevue Baptist Church, Cordova, Tennessee. Used by permission.

16. Peggy Perkins, former elementary school principal and former children's director, author's questionnaire.

17. Dr. Edwin Young, *The Winning Walk* (Broadcast Ministry of Second Baptist Church, Houston, Tex.), 13 November 2003. Used by permission.

18. Dr. James Merritt, sermon on parenting at First Baptist Church, Snellville, Georgia, 20 October 2002.

19. Marsolini, *Blended Families,* 112.

20. Daisy Hepburn, speaking at Bellevue Baptist Church, Memphis, Tennessee.

21. Van Snider, M.D., author's questionnaire.

CHAPTER 6

1. Anne Taylor as quoted in *God's Little Devotional Book for Moms,* 236.

2. Shannon Fife as quoted in *God's Little Devotional Book for Moms,* 258.

3. Bertha Smith, *Go Home and Tell* (Nashville, Tenn.: Broadman & Holman, 1995), 224.

4. Ibid.

5. Seminar by Major Ian Thomas, Founder and Director of The Torchbearers given at Bellevue Baptist Church, Cordova, Tennessee.

6. Van Snider, M.D., author's questionnaire.

7. Dr. Adrian Rogers, speaking at Bellevue Baptist Church, Cordova, Tennessee. Used by permission.

8. Nancy Binkley, mother of three, educational consultant, and Bible Study Fellowship leader, author's questionnaire.

9. *The Women's Study Bible,* 2069.

10. Batten et al., *Tough-Minded Parenting,* 53.

CHAPTER 7

1. *Noah Webster's First Edition of An American Dictionary of the English Language* (San Francisco, Calif.; Foundation for American Christian Education, 1967).

2. James Dobson, *Bringing Up Boys,* 250.

3. Ibid.

4. George Barna, "Parents Accept Responsibility for Their Child's Spiritual Development but Struggle with Effectiveness," 6 May 2003, *Barna Online Research.* Used by permission.

5. Cos H. Davis, Jr., *Children and the Christian Faith,* rev. ed. (Nashville, Tenn.: Broadman Press, 1990), 46.

6. George Barna, "Beliefs: Salvation," 1994.

7. *The Women's Study Bible,* 877.

8. John Witherspoon, (1723–1794), source unknown.

9. "Time with God" *The New Testament for Busy People* (Dallas, Tex.: Word, 1991), 181; excerpt from Patrick Morley's *I Surrender* (Word, 1990).

10. Ibid.

11. Josh McDowell and Bob Hostetler, *Right from Wrong* (Nashville, Tenn.: W. Publishing, 1994), 91. All rights reserved.

12. Smalley and Trent, *The Gift of Honor,* 117.

13. Batten, et al., "Prime Time TV—a Clear and Present Danger," *Tough-Minded Parenting,* 92.

14. McDowell and Hostetler, *Right from Wrong,* 35.

15. Henry Blackaby and Roy Edgemon, *The Ways of God* (Nashville, Tenn.: Broadman & Holman, 2000), 47.

16. George Barna, "Parents Accept Responsibility," 6 May 2003, *Barna Online Research.* Used by permission.

17. VanderSteeg, author's questionnaire.

18. McDowell and Hostetler, *Right from Wrong,* 7.

19. Dobson, *Bringing Up Boys,* 248.

20. Ibid., 248–49.

21. Ibid., 249.

CHAPTER 8

1. Henry and Richard Blackaby, *Experiencing God Day by Day Devotional* (Nashville, Tenn.: Broadman & Holman, 1998), 280.

2. Paul W. Powell, *A Faith that Sings* (Nashville, Tenn.: Broadman Press, l989), 101.

3. Sidlow Baxter, *Awake My Heart,* 245, public domain.

CHAPTER 9

1. Davis, *Children and the Christian Faith,* 46.

2. Henry Blackaby and Claude V. King, *Experiencing God* (Nashville, Tenn.: LifeWay Press, 1990), 98.

3. J. B. Phillips, *Letters to Young Churches* (New York: The Macmillan Company, 1958), 27.

4. Rick Warren, *The Purpose-Driven Life* (Grand Rapids, Mich.: Zondervan, 2002), 81.

5. VanderSteeg, author's questionnaire.

6. George Barna, "Teens Evaluate the Church-Based Ministry They Received as Children," 8 July 2003, *Barna Research Online.* Used by permission.

7. Ibid.

8. Taken from *The Baptist Record, Journal of the Mississippi Baptist Convention,* vol. 127, no. 38 (30 October 2003), 1.

9. Josh McDowell, *Beyond Beliefs to Convictions* (Wheaton, Ill.: Tyndale House Publishers, 2002), 5–7. Used by permission.

CHAPTER 10

1. Dr. Howard Hendricks, Family Seminar at Bellevue Baptist Church, Memphis, Tennessee, 1976.

2. Material taken from *My Utmost for His Highest* by Oswald Chambers, edited by James Reimann, copyright © 1992 by Oswald Chambers Publications Assn., Ltd. Original edition copyright © 1935 by Dodd Mead & Co., renewed 1963 by the Oswald Chambers Publications Assn., Ltd. Used by permission of Discovery House Publishers, Box 3566, Grand Rapids, MI 49501. All rights reserved.

3. Marjorie Holmes, "If Only," *Lord, Let Me Love* (Garden City, N.Y.: Doubleday and Company, Inc., 1978), 194.

4. Kay Arthur, *Lord, Only You Can Change Me* (Colorado Springs, Colo.: Waterbrook Press, 2000, 92–93). Used by permission.

5. Matthew Henry, *A Commentary on the Whole Bible,* vol. 1 (Old Tappan, N.J.: Fleming H. Revell Company, 1979), 865.

6. Arthur Cleveland Bent, "Familiar Birds: Golden Eagle Collection," *Life Histories of North American Birds,* Electronic Book Collection, 7.

7. Jerry and Mary White, *When Your Kids Aren't Kids Anymore* (Colorado Springs, Co.: Navpress, 1989), 8.

8. Author Unknown.

9. Joyce Rogers, *The Secret of a Woman's Influence* (Nashville, Tenn.: Broadman Press, 1988), 56.

10. Sarah Maddox and Patti Webb, *A Woman's Garden of Prayer* (Nashville, Tenn.: Broadman & Holman, 2002), 110.

11. Ibid.

CONCLUSION

1. McDowell and Hostetler, *Right from Wrong,* 12–13.

2. Dobson, *Bringing Up Boys,* 250.

3. Ibid.

4. Ibid.

5. Pat Brown, Christian counselor and mother, author's questionnaire.

6. VanderSteeg, author's questionnaire.

Appendix A

1. *Random House Dictionary of the English Language,* s.v. "discernment."

2. William Barclay, *The Daily Study Bible: The Letters to the Galatians and Ephesians* (Philadelphia, Penn.: The Westminster Press, l956), 153. Used by permission.

3. Ibid., 153–154.

4. *Noah Webster's First Edition of an American Dictionary of the English Language,* s.v. "diligence."

5. Ibid., s.v. "dedicate."

Appendix B

1. *Random House Dictionary of the English Language,* s.v. "educate."

2. Peggy Perkins, former elementary school principal and former children's director, author's questionnaire.

3. Stanley, *How to Keep Your Kids on Your Team,* 105.

Appendix C

1. Dan Dehaan, *Intercepted by Christ* (Lilburn Ga.: Crossroads Books, 1980), 53.